D0064821

Biodegradable

Number Twelve:
Environmental History Series
Martin V. Melosi, General Editor

Biodegradable

DETERGENTS AND THE ENVIRONMENT

William McGucken

Texas A&M University Press
College Station

Library of Congress Cataloging-in-Publication Data

McGucken, William.
   Biodegradable : detergents and the environment / William McGucken.
—1st ed.
      p.   cm.—(Environmental history series : no. 12)
   Includes bibliographical references and index.
   ISBN 0-89096-479-3
   1. Detergent pollution of rivers, lakes, etc.   2. Detergents, Synthetic.
   3. Synthetic detergents industry.   I. Title.   II. Series.
   TD427.D4M38   1991
   363.73′8—dc20   90-29035
                                                              CIP

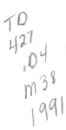

For Emilia

Contents

Acknowledgments

I wish to thank Howard Stephens and Brian Arbuckle, colleagues at the University of Akron, for their useful comments on an early draft of the book, and Martin Melosi and Craig Colten for their valuable suggestions for improving a later draft. I also want to thank Joel Tarr, who readily supplied copies of his and his coauthors' articles on the historical development in the United States of technologies for the management of domestic wastewaters. I am grateful to Mia O'Connor for her excellent typing of the various drafts of the book, Emilia Nadel McGucken for her help in numerous ways, and the University of Akron for a Faculty Summer Fellowship and its support and encouragement in other ways.

Biodegradable

Introduction

The environmental movement of recent decades within the United States has been depicted by Samuel P. Hays as being rooted in vast social changes that followed World War II.[1] According to Hays, the movement "differed markedly" from the conservation movement of the early twentieth century. "The conservation movement was an effort on the part of leaders in science, technology, and government to bring about more efficient development of physical resources. The environmental movement, on the other hand, was far more widespread and popular, involving public values that stressed the quality of human experience and hence of the human environment."[2] Hays sees the environmental movement as having evolved through three stages, with each "giving rise to distinctive substantive issues, organized environmental action, governmental response, and balance of power between environmental advocates and their opponents." The initial issues, which "shaped debate between 1957 and 1965," concerned "natural-environment values in outdoor recreation, wildlands, and open space." The second stage, running from 1965 to 1972, was dominated by concern about pollution, particularly water and air pollution. Finally, the principal subjects of the third phase beginning in the early 1970s were "toxic chemicals, energy, and the possibilities for social, economic, and political decentralization."[3]

Writing more than a decade before Hays, J. Clarence Davies III and Barbara S. Davies portrayed in post–World War II America both a widespread public concern about environmental pollution and a determination at the federal level of government to abate pollution.[4] To them the country's booming postwar economy, with its expanding industrial production and growing consumer consumption, together with an increasing population underlay the burgeoning pollution problem. Barry Commoner argued that new production technologies accompanying the increasing production were key contributing elements in pollution.[5]

Affluence had led to increased pollution, but in the Davieses' view it had also underlain a public desire, and the federal government's ability, to combat pollution. Increased leisure time, coupled with a demand for recreational resources and aesthetic satisfaction, fueled public desire, and national wealth provided the federal government the resources necessary for action.[6] In digging deeper for the roots of "environment impulses," Hays argues that new values and new ways of looking at ourselves emerged to generate new preferences. He claims that these developments were characteristic of all advanced industrial societies, not just the United States, and that they reflected two major and widespread social changes. One, parallel to the Davieses' view, is "associated with the search for standards of living beyond necessities and conveniences to include amenities made possible by considerable increases in personal and social 'real income.' "[7] The other arose from "advancing levels of education which have generated values associated with personal creativity and self-development, involvement with natural environments, physical and mental fitness and wellness and political autonomy and efficacy." For Hays, environmental values and objectives are integral to these social changes.

As to values, new aesthetic and health ones "constituted much of the roots of environmental concern."[8] Regarding aesthetic values, "an increasing portion of the American people came to value natural environments as an integral part of their rising standard of living. They sought out many types of such places to experience, to explore, enjoy and protect: high mountains and forests, wetlands, ocean shores, swamplands, wild and scenic rivers, deserts, pine barrens, remnants of the original prairies, places of relatively clean air and water, more limited 'natural areas.' " As for health values, Hays sees a new view of well-being as an equally significant innovation—"health less as freedom from illness and more as physical and mental fitness, of feeling well, of optimal capability for exercising one's physical and mental powers." Threats to these new values led to demands for public action resulting in some of the "most celebrated environmental battles: power and petrochemical plant siting, hardrock mining and strip mining, chemicals in the workplace and in underground drinking water supplies, energy transmission lines and pipelines."

In addition to changes in values Hays, like Commoner, emphasizes changes in the magnitude and form of threats from modern technology in explaining the historical timing of the environmental movement. Technology, notes Hays, "was applied in increasing scale and scope, from enormous draglines in strip mining, to 1,000-megawatt electric generating plants and 'energy parks,' to superports and large-scale petrochemical plants to 765-kilovolt transmission lines."[9] There was also "the vast increase in the use and release into the environment of chemicals, relatively contained and generating a chemical 'sea around us' which many people considered to be a long-run hazard that was out of control."

The fact that pollution of the environment affected all citizens made it a popular political issue, and Congress was moved to enact various pieces of anti-pollution legislation.[10] The Water Pollution Control Act of 1948, which would be amended in 1956 and again in 1961, was the first major piece of federal water pollution control legislation. Two subjects—federal enforcement powers and financial assistance to municipalities for the construction of sewage treatment plants—dominated the debates associated with the act and its amendments.[11] The original act directed the Public Health Service to develop or adopt comprehensive programs for the abatement of water pollution problems in cooperation with the states, interstate agencies, municipalities and industry.[12] These programs were to be developed for surface waters and groundwaters and were to take into account all potential uses of water, including public water supply; recreational, agricultural, and industrial uses; and the maintenance of aquatic life. The act authorized federal loans to municipalities for the construction of sewage treatment plants. It also provided for federal enforcement, but only on interstate waters, defined as waters that flow across, or form a part of, the boundaries between two or more states.[13] The Federal Water Pollution Control Act Amendments of 1956 extended and strengthened the Water Pollution Control Act.[14] The amended act, which authorized federal grants for the construction of sewage treatment plants, was to be administered by the Surgeon General of the Public Health Service under the supervision and direction of the Secretary of the Department of Health, Education, and Welfare (HEW). In 1961 Congress again amended the Water Pollution Control Act, transferring responsibility for enforcing the act to the Secretary of HEW; increasing grants to municipalities for the construction of sewage treatment plants; and extending federal enforcement authority to cover navigable as well as interstate waters.[15]

Joel Tarr has written extensively about the development of technologies for the management of domestic wastewaters in the United States.[16] During the period 1800–80, which he calls the pre-sewer period, human wastes were deposited primarily in cesspools and privy vaults. When these receptacles were emptied, the wastes were either used as fertilizer by farmers or dumped into water courses or onto vacant lands. During the same period many cities introduced running water—by 1860 there were 136 water works in the United States—but no city simultaneously provided any new means of removing the increased volume of wastewater. Municipal authorities apparently assumed that the prevailing means of wastewater disposal—street gutters and cesspools—would suffice. But they did not, and the overflow problem was compounded by the introduction of the water closet, which by 1880 had been installed in approximately one-third of urban households.[17] Some cities had storm water sewers, but the law generally forbade the disposing of human excrement in them.

During the last decades of the nineteenth century it became increasingly apparent that the solution of the burgeoning wastewater problem required the installation of sewers that transported wastes by water carriage. The question became whether human wastes and surface runoff from precipitation should be carried in one or in separate pipe channels. By the end of the century larger cities generally favored the former option, the combined system, and disposed of domestic wastes and runoff together.[18] Smaller cities and towns tended to opt for separate systems, although generally building only sanitary sewers and allowing precipitation to run off on the ground. In both cases domestic wastes were usually disposed of in nearby water courses, and the resulting pollution frequently led to epidemics of typhoid fever in downstream communities drawing their water supplies from these water courses.

The general municipal response to this latest problem was to treat water extracted from polluted rivers by filtration and chlorination before use, rather than to install sewage treatment facilities that would only directly benefit downstream communities. Consequently, as late as 1930 some 45 million people were served by water-treatment facilities as compared to one third as many served by sewage-treatment plants.[19] During the 1930s the United States federal government, through the Works Progress Administration, began to foster sewage-treatment plant construction.[20] By 1938 the creation of some thirteen hundred new plants had raised the population served by treatment facilities to some 39 million people.[21] In the postwar period federal support for further construction was administered under the Water Pollution Control Act, and the population served by treatment facilities rose to some 76 million in 1957 and 104 million by 1962.[22] By the late 1940s the most advanced treatment plants subjected sewage to both primary and secondary treatments (described in chapter two), although as late as 1962 secondary treatment was far from being universally practiced.

The case study presented here forms part of post–World War II American environmental history. More specifically, at first glance it might appear to fall within Hays's second stage of the environmental movement. The study concerns the unanticipated pollution of water by one of the new technologies discussed by Commoner, synthetic detergents. As federal legislation to abate water pollution was being enacted, and as the consequent construction of sewage treatment plants proceeded, the new detergents were being expelled in increasing quantities into urban and rural wastewater treatment systems from increasing numbers of other popular new technological creations, domestic laundry- and dish-washing machines. Even the most advanced sewage treatment plants, those employing secondary treatment, proved incapable of effectively treating detergents and consequently of preventing them from polluting surface and underground waters. The problem constituted a major and novel challenge to treatment plant operators and sanitary engineers. The paradox was that achieving human cleanliness entailed fouling the environment.

This study explores the various processes that culminated in the rejection in the United States during the early 1960s of synthetic detergents of low biodegradability and their replacement by highly biodegradable ones. These processes involved the activities of diverse groups—operators of sewage treatment and water purification plants, sanitary engineers, academic and industrial scientists, industrial managers, government officials, and state and national legislators. Although the study focuses on the American experience, it also sketches the contemporary parallel experiences of Great Britain and, to a lesser degree, West Germany.

The book is intended also as a case study of a more general issue, namely, the social control of technology. In an earlier book I have shown that during the 1930s British scientists debated the question of who in a democratic society is responsible for the uses to which science and technology are put. In the summer of 1938 they concluded that not only scientists and engineers but all members of society share this responsibility.[23] Accepting that as a sound conclusion, the question then becomes how this responsibility is met in actual practice. Society chooses the technologies it wants, but how does it go about doing so? While all new technologies probably hurt someone to some degree, generally they have been passively accepted and put to work with much, or little, fanfare. Occasionally, however, and increasingly so in the second half of this century, the adoption of a new technology has encountered opposition.[24] The technology generates opponents as its use becomes a matter of controversy. Such instances provide opportunities for examining the social processes of choosing technologies; the mildly controversial, widespread pollution by synthetic detergents, which began during the late 1940s, gave rise to one such instance.

A single case study cannot be expected to yield any permanent general conclusions regarding the processes of the social choice of technology. However, it can be used to explore tentative general observations concerning these processes. From my reading of relevant literature, it would appear that controversial technologies can meet with four distinct types of opposition. The least severe of the four does not occur in the public arena; following Allan Mazur, I shall call it in-house opposition.[25] Here, the new technology is opposed, or at least questioned, by some technologists who have professional knowledge of it. The opposition, or questioning, proceeds unknown to the lay public, which may never become aware of it if the particular problem is resolved. Unresolved problems, however, sooner or later emerge into the lay public's view via the news media, and it is there that the other three types of opposition are expressed. Two of these fall within the law and the third outside it. Although the three types may be expressed simultaneously, it seems generally true that in the public arena opposition initially takes the form of persuading government, whether at the national, local, or some intermediate level, to take action against the technology in question. The appeal for government action may take a variety of forms; it may come from individuals—either citizens or legislators—or from organizations; and it may involve public demonstrations. If in the eyes of some opponents, government is slow to act, or it takes some unsatisfactory action, they intensify their opposition by going to court to oppose the technology they consider undesirable.[26] Some few, unhappy even with a court ruling, will go beyond the law and resort to the most severe form of opposition, civil disobedience.[27]

This case study of technological choice affords an opportunity to examine the first two types of opposition. The study begins with an outline of the history of the manufacture of soap and synthetic detergents, showing the rapid growth in production of the latter and their widespread substitution for soap, particularly for domestic laundry purposes, immediately after World War II. As this transformation occurred, sewage treatment plant operators throughout the United States reported unprecedented foaming in their plants. They pointed to the new detergents as the cause of the foaming, which was soon also occurring on rivers and lakes used as sources of domestic water supply. The detergent industry denied that detergents caused the foaming; but an independent investigation carried out by sanitary engineers at the Massachusetts Institute of Technology demonstrated that surfactants—in particular the leading surfactant, ABS (alkyl benzene sulfonate)—were the cause. The industry's subsequent study of the fate of ABS in sewage treatment plants confirmed that a substantial percentage of it passed undegraded through even the best plants into receiving waters. Where cesspools were used, groundwater was also found from 1958 to contain ABS. The public's realization that ABS could be present in its drinking water heightened its concern about the detergent pollution problem. The industry studied the toxicity of ABS and determined that ABS posed no threat to human health in the concentrations found in surface and ground waters. It attempted to downplay the detergent pollution problem, calling it merely an aesthetic one. But the ploy did not placate a public that did not want unsightly foam on its rivers, lakes, and tap water, a public that was uneasy about the possible effects on human health of lifetime ingestion of even low concentrations of a synthetic material.

By the late 1950s, as the U.S. public was beginning to express opposition to pollution by synthetic detergents, the country's detergent industry knew that it would have to seek a replacement for ABS. The industry looked to Britain, where pollution by detergents had also been experienced. The British government had from 1953 intervened by setting up official committees, including industry representatives, to examine and seek a solution to the problem. In West Germany the Bundestag in 1961, preferring compulsion to cooperation, passed a law requiring the industry to market from October, 1964, only detergents that were more than 80 percent degradable. The Bundestag's action appealed to a few Democrats in the U.S. Congress, who early in 1963 introduced bills banning the manufacture of nondegradable detergents within the United States from mid-1965. The sponsors regarded the bills as part of the ongoing federal attack on water pollution, presenting them as amendments to the Water Pollution Control Act. The U.S. detergent industry vigorously opposed the bills, arguing that it would be best if it were allowed to solve the problem voluntarily; it initially claimed it could do so by the end of 1965. The Congress was persuaded by the industry's arguments.

By the time bills had been introduced into the U.S. Congress, a decade of research by the international detergent industry in Britain, West Germany, and the United States had finally yielded a solution to the problem through the development in the United States during 1962–63 of the technology of molecular sieves. Utilizing this technology the United States detergent industry produced the highly degradable surfactant LAS (linear alkyl sulfonate), with which it had replaced ABS and solved the detergent pollution problem by June 30, 1965—significantly, the date specified in the Congressional bills for the elimination of nondegradable detergents. The bills speeded the substitution of ABS by LAS in the United States, but it had been the earlier governmental actions in Britain and West Germany, together with the U.S. industry's anticipation of governmental action, that had spurred the development of LAS.

The different ways of tackling the problem of detergent pollution by the three governments concerned—the British cooperative, the West German legislative, and the American voluntary—are found to be characteristic of the countries' traditions in the area of public policy. Despite the differences, in each country the public had, through government, successfully pressured industry to produce an acceptable surfactant, one with minimal environmental effect.

In assessing the impact in the United States of the environmental movement, whose birth he dates, in contrast to Samuel P. Hays, from Earth Day in April of 1970, Barry Commoner recently observed that the decade or more of effort to improve the quality of the environment has taught a simple lesson: "pollution levels can be reduced enough to at least approach the goal of elimination only if the production or the use of the offending substance is halted."[28] In the case of each of the successful environmental improvements that Commoner notes—the sharp reduction of mercury in surface waters, and the reduction of lead, DDT and similar chlorinated pesticides, and radioactive fallout from nuclear-bomb tests in the environment generally—such termi-

nation has meant an alteration in technology. The replacement of ABS by
LAS was another cause of environmental improvement that lends credence to
Commoner's points—the elimination of an offending substance through a
change in technology.

Commoner believes that corporations cannot be relied upon to make the
proper technological choices—the key in his view to solving environmental
problems—and argues that technological choices should be made by societies
and their governments. He wishes that the American environmental movement would embrace these ideas. Commoner considers conventional environ-
mentalism to be preoccupied with controlling emissions of pollutants rather
than with changing the production processes that generate them. Largely responsible for this preoccupation, he believes, is "the conviction, powerfully
embedded in American society, that the decisions that determine what is produced and by what technological means ought to remain in private, corporate
hands."[29] That conviction is seen in the present study; but the detergent industry was not without a sense of social responsibility. Nevertheless, the
American public, through its government, pressured the industry to choose
detergents of high biodegradability over ones of low biodegradability. The
means of technological choice advocated by Commoner was effective in this
instance.

Finally, I have noted how Commoner and Hays differ as to when the environmental movement began. Commoner takes Earth Day to be its beginning, the "most common interpretation" according to Hays.[30] Hays views
Earth Day as much a result as a cause, pointing out that it occurred "after a
decade or more of evolution in attitudes and programs without which it would
not have been possible." Deciding just when the environmental movement
began has much to do with how one chooses to define the movement itself,
particularly in regard to the extent of public involvement in it. Although I
favor Hays's view of an evolving movement with different stages, I cannot
accept his depiction of a second stage running from 1965 to 1972 and dominated by concern about water and air pollution. Water pollution had been a
concern of the U.S. Congress from the 1930s.[31] The Water Pollution Control
Act was enacted in 1948 and then significantly amended in 1956. This is a
year before Hays says his first phase of the environmental movement, concerned with quite different issues, began. The Water Pollution Control Act
was amended again in 1961, and the activities of the early 1960s that form
the subject of this study were part of still further attempts in 1963–64, eventually successful in 1965 (when Hays's second stage begins), to amend the
Act. In light of these considerations, concern about water pollution must be
seen as having been central to the environmental movement from its beginning.

I

The Coming of Synthetic Detergents

The decade following World War II witnessed a revolution in the manufacture and use of domestic cleaning materials. Soap, which had been the primary cleaning agent for centuries, was superseded in many of its diverse uses by synthetic detergents. First produced in Germany during World War I, synthetic detergents were manufactured in the United States from the early 1930s; but they were not widely used, in part because they were several times as expensive as soap and unsatisfactory for laundry purposes. With the introduction of sodium tripolyphosphate as a "builder" immediately after World War II, all-purpose synthetic detergents appeared. At the same time, the American detergent industry, utilizing technical advances made in the petroleum industry during the war, produced new and cheaper detergents, those incorporating alkyl benzene sulfonate in particular, from petroleum. By 1953 the production by weight of detergents had risen in the United States to equal that of soap, which was in decline. Five years later, more than twice as much synthetic detergent as soap was being manufactured, and the amount of detergent was rapidly approaching the maximum amount of soap that had been made towards the end of World War II. The successful new synthetic detergents responsible for soap's decline included specialized laundry detergents, such as Tide, Fab, and Surf, which incorporated sodium tripolyphosphate and alkyl benzene sulfonate.

Soap had been used for centuries before the French chemist M. E. Chevreul in the early nineteenth century first provided a clear understanding of the chemical nature and reactions of the raw materials—fats, fatty oils, and alkalis—used in its manufacture.[1] In the soap industry of the twentieth century the most generally used animal oils were tallow and grease, while the most commonly employed vegetable oils were coconut, cottonseed, corn, soya, palm, palm kernel, and olive.[2]

The most useful property of soaps is that of greatly enhancing the cleaning, or detergent, power of water in which they are dissolved. Until the advent of synthetic detergents, soaps were the only chemically inactive substances that could improve the cleaning power of water. They are especially good cleaning agents when used in soft, warm, alkaline water.[3] However, they have two serious shortcomings. One is that in acid or even neutral solutions, soaps are converted into fatty acids, which have no detergent power. Thus soap cannot be used in industrial cleaning processes where acids are present. The other shortcoming of soap is that it is very inefficient in hard water. The calcium and magnesium ions of hard water react with soap to form a greasy scum; and only after all the calcium and magnesium have reacted in this way will additional soap render the solution a cleaning one. To illustrate the magnitude of this problem, water of average hardness contains the equivalent of only one hundred parts of calcium carbonate to one million parts of water. For such water to be as efficient in cleaning as distilled water, approximately 10 percent more soap is required. The larger part of the United States is supplied with water that contains at least one hundred parts of calcium or magnesium per million.[4]

Soaps were the earliest used members of a group of substances eventually known as surface-active agents. These agents have the property of being able to orient themselves at the interface of two surfaces in such a way that they act as coupling agents bringing the surfaces into more intimate contact. For example, the interface could be that of a liquid and a gas, such as water and air, in which case the surface-active agent would produce a foam. Surface-active agents may also possess the properties of wetting (that is, permitting penetration of a water solution into capillaries by lowering the interfacial tension), dispersing (separating agglomerated particles), and emulsifying (linking oil or dirt particles with water molecules). A particular agent may possess one of these last three properties to a greater degree than the other two, and so may be regarded primarily as a wetting, dispersing, or emulsifying agent. An agent, on the other hand, which possesses wetting, dispersing, and emulsifying properties to comparable degrees is a cleaning agent, and is called a detergent. Soaps, being simultaneously wetting, dispersing, and emulsifying agents are therefore surface-active agents and detergents.[5]

Certain other surface-active agents, which also possess all three properties, are the so-called synthetic detergents. The origin of this confusing term is obscure. The term is confusing in that soap itself is a man-made, or synthetic, as opposed to naturally occurring, detergent. Perhaps the best meaning that can be given to the term "synthetic detergent" is this: a cleaning agent free of the shortcomings of soap, i.e., an agent that can clean equally well in acidic or alkaline solution, and in hard or soft water. As will be seen, synthetic detergents have been made from a great variety of raw materials and are of widely varying chemical composition. By some they have been called "soapless soaps" and by others "syndets." In this book I have generally followed common practice and simply used the term "synthetic detergent" in the sense of a cleaning agent other than soap.

Soaps and detergents perform the primary cleaning of the washing action in the same way: through the reduction of surface tensions. The cleaning process consists of thoroughly wetting the soiling matter and the article being washed, removing the matter from the article, and maintaining the matter in a stable solution or suspension. Soaps and detergents increase the wetting ability of water so that it may more readily penetrate into fabrics and reach the soiling matter. Each molecule of the cleaning agent may be considered to be a long chain, with one end being hydrophilic (water-attracting) and the other hydrophobic (water-avoiding and soil-attracting). Detergents excel in these special properties to effect soil removal. The soil-attracting ends of detergent molecules are attracted to a soil particle and surround it. At the same time the water-attracting ends are pulling the molecules and the soil particles away from the fabric and into the wash water. When combined with the mechanical agitation of the washing machine, this action enables a soap or detergent to remove soil, suspend it, and keep it from redepositing on clothes.[6]

Following the pioneering work of Chevreul, knowledge of the chemistry of fats and fatty oils and fatty acids advanced rapidly. One result was the discovery of the so-called sulfonated fatty oils in 1834. When animal or vegetable fats are treated with concentrated sulfuric acid and subsequently neutralized with caustic soda, soluble oils are obtained. In water these products form clear, brilliant solutions that have pronounced wetting and penetrating properties.[7] One of them, sulfonated castor oil, was first commercially produced in 1860. It became widely known as Turkey-red oil from its use as an excellent wetting agent for fabrics that were to be dyed the color Turkey-red with madder root. Although Turkey-red oil was most effective in spreading the dye evenly on fabric, it had limited detergent power.[8] But it was the first commercially used synthetic surface-active agent. It was followed by many other sulfonated oils prepared from a variety of animal and vegetable fats.[9] For many industrial purposes, such as wetting, the sulfonated oils were found to be superior to soap.

The first attempts to make synthetic detergents occurred in Germany during World War I after the Allied blockade had led to a serious shortage of fats and oils. German chemists attempted to develop soap substitutes from materials other than fats. On October 23, 1917, Fritz Gunther of Badische Anilin-und-Soda-Fabrik filed a patent for a detergent made from raw materials derived from coal tar, abundant in Germany, and from other nonfat sources.

Gunther's work led to the production of a series of short-chain alkyl naphthalene sulfonic acids made by coupling propyl or butyl alcohols with naphthalene followed by sulfonation. The first synthetic detergent was the sodium salt of diisopropylnaphthalene sulfonic acid. It was marketed under the trade name Nekal from 1925 by I. G. Farbenindustrie, which had absorbed Badische Anilin-und-Soda-Fabrik just after the war. However, Nekal proved to be only a fair to moderately good detergent, and was to enjoy a longer life as a satisfactory wetting agent. It was also used as an effective emulsifying agent for hydrocarbons and tar oils.[10]

During the 1920s the German textile industry, prompted by economic considerations, began to explore ways of reducing its costs of using soap in the hard waters prevalent in many parts of Germany. Thus once again German chemists turned their attention to developing substitutes for soap.[11] Their investigations led to the recognition that the cause of soap's shortcomings in hard water lay in the active carboxyl group (COOH) of the soap molecule. It was this group that reacted with the calcium and magnesium ions of hard water to destroy the cleaning power of soap.[12] One approach to the problem was to seek some means of "blocking" this group by tying it up in a chemical compound so that it could not react further. However, the carboxyl group is the hydrophilic group of the soaps, and a surface-active compound has to have a hydrophilic group.[13] The problem was solved by an ingenious choice of compound to "block" the carboxyl group—namely, a compound consisting of a short hydrocarbon chain having a reactive group at either end. One group was so chosen as to be capable of reacting readily with the carboxyl group, while the other was the strongly hydrophilic sulfonic acid group ($-SO_3H$). Even more useful was the hydrophilic sulfate ester group ($-OSO_3H$), in which the sulfur atom is linked to the carbon chain through an oxygen atom.[14]

The German firm of H. T. Bohme produced the first group of commercial synthetic detergent products—the Avirol series, sulfuric acid esters of butyl ricinoleic esters in 1928. Two years later they introduced a series of fatty alcohol sulfates under the trade name Gardinol. These compounds were made by sulfating fatty alcohols obtained by the high pressure hydrogenation of fatty acids.[15]

During the same period, I. G. Farbenindustrie took a different approach to solving the problem of soap's inefficiency in hard water. They wanted to eliminate rather than block the carboxyl group, and they concentrated their investigations on the esters of fatty acids. Beginning in 1930 they marketed in Germany the Igepon A series, which comprised fatty acid esters of hydroxyethanesulfonic acid. This series proved too unstable for many applications and was succeeded in Germany in 1931 by the Igepon T series. These products represented yet another approach to the elimination of the carboxyl group. They were amides, derivatives of taurine, and were sufficiently stable for most textile processing work.[16]

The first synthetic detergent to arrive in the United States was Gardinol, introduced under the sponsorship of National Aniline in 1930, the year in which it appeared in Europe. The American subsidiary of I. G. Farbenindustrie, the General Aniline Works, began producing Igepon A in 1931 and Igepon T the following year.[17] The introduction of Gardinol and the Igepons was the beginning of the synthetic detergent industry in the United States. At the time synthetic detergents were used primarily in shampoo preparations, but they also served as the active constituents of the first so-called soapless detergent powders, such as Dreft, the nation's first packaged detergent washing product designed for dishes and fine fabrics.[18]

Charles Wilson observes in *The History of Unilever* that in the detergent industry "the most significant change of the thirties was the growth of the trade in soap powders. Closely linked with this development was the appearance in the middle thirties of soapless detergent powders designed for all kinds of washing purposes."[19] The introduction of Dreft was a result of Procter and Gamble's investigation of the new types of detergents. In the early 1930s, Procter and Gamble's idea scouts had studied the recent synthetic detergent developments in Germany, and shortly afterward the company acquired a license to manufacture and sell alcohol sulfate synthetic detergents for household and laundry purposes. After more than a year of laboratory tests, Procter and Gamble in 1933 introduced Dreft into three towns in hard water areas near its home base of Cincinnati, Ohio—Oxford and Troy, Ohio, and Crawfordsville, Indiana. To promote Dreft, Procter and Gamble advertised extensively in newspapers and conducted house-to-house sampling campaigns. The company strove to make the product, a white granular substance, and its package as familiar as possible. The attractive package, made similar in size to familiar soap packages, carried simple but complete washing directions. It also claimed that Dreft made "5 times as much suds as soap, 12 times faster;" and one newspaper advertisement began in large type with the sentence, "Well, I never saw such suds in Crawfordsville."[20] Prompted in part by such advertising, the public had mistakenly come to accept that the quantity of suds was an indicator of the cleaning power of the wash liquid—the more, the better. Special Dreft salesmen provided cold water sudsing demonstrations in stores. A soap solution was placed in one bottle and a solution of Dreft in another, and a few quick shakes revealed the difference in suds arising from the two solutions. Attending housewives received full-sized, free samples of Dreft.

A limiting factor in the sale of the alcohol sulfates was their high cost as compared with that of soap. In 1934 they were from four to five times more expensive. Nevertheless, the use of Dreft spread in hard water areas, and by 1936 it was threatening the trade in soap flakes in those localities.[21] However, as Dreft was not effective in removing heavy soilage, it was not recommended for the family wash.

During World War II various instances drew attention to the valuable properties of synthetic detergents. One example was the underground "Rock" laundry at Gibraltar, where the garrison's hospital linen and clothing were washed with synthetic detergents, thereby enabling the washing to be done with seawater, fresh water being required only for rinsing. In the United States the increase in production of synthetic detergents was due largely to the requirements of the fighting services; for instance, ships that were at sea for long periods required detergents that could be used effectively in seawater. In both the United States and the United Kingdom, large quantities of synthetic detergents were used for compounding with fatty acid soaps to produce the so-called General Purpose Soap, which could be used in seawater. Some forty-eight million tablets of general purpose soap were supplied to Britain's fighting forces, mainly in the Far East.[22]

At the end of 1946, Procter and Gamble introduced their new synthetic product, Tide, which was to initiate a revolution in the U.S. detergent industry.[23] Although it would soon become known solely as a laundry detergent, Tide was the first all-purpose synthetic detergent designed to do the entire family wash as well as a wide variety of other household tasks, including washing the dishes. Tide had sufficient "cleaning muscles," as they said in the industry, to compete with heavy-duty soap products in most household tasks and to surpass them in the cleaning of clothes.[24]

The search for an all-purpose detergent had not been an easy one. Tests showed that the cleaning ability of detergents could be improved by adding so-called builders, similar to those known to improve the performance of soap. Builders are compounds, including carbonates and silicates, which soften water by deactivating hardness minerals and provide a desirable level of alkalinity, which aids in cleaning. However, the builders left clothes harsh and stiff, because they reacted with hard water to form insoluble granular deposits that adhered to the clothes. It was not until the early 1940s that researchers with Procter and Gamble found a satisfactory builder, sodium tripolyphosphate.[25] It proved effective in removing soil and left clothes soft and free of objectionable deposits. The advantage of phosphates is that they combine with the hardness minerals, calcium and magnesium, to form a soluble complex that is carried off in the wash water.

Unable to build the necessary plant or to secure an adequate supply of raw materials during wartime, Procter and Gamble could not manufacture sodium tripolyphosphate in bulk until immediately after World War II.[26] The company then seized the initiative and vigorously promoted Tide with large-scale advertising. Thanks to this effort, and to Tide's performance, by 1949 Tide had become the leading domestic detergent in the United States.[27] It was effective in hard or soft water, for dishwashing or heavy-duty laundering. Soft water required about the same amount of Tide as soap flakes, but hard water required only about half as much Tide as soap.[28] A full-page, colored advertisement in the January, 1950, issue of *Good Housekeeping* proclaimed that "Tide gives oceans of suds in *hardest* water" and boasted that "Tide gets clothes cleaner than any other washday product you can buy!"

The surface-active agent or "surfactant," to employ the detergent industry's term, in Tide, as in Dreft, was a sulfated fatty alcohol, derived in the case of Tide from coconut oil. When coconut oil was either too expensive or not available, Tide was made with substantial quantities of a significant new type of surfactant, alkyl aryl sulfonate.[29]

During the 1930s research teams, particularly in the United States and Germany, had explored again, as German researchers had done during World War I and the 1920s, the possibility of using non-fatty raw materials for the manufacture of synthetic detergents.[30] Chemists saw mineral oil as an obvious alternative to fatty oil as a source of long-chain hydrocarbons. Moreover, mineral oil was comparatively inexpensive, and in terms of world production much more abundant than fatty oil. However, paraffin hydrocarbons were well-known by organic chemists to be not very reactive, and the eventual large-scale development of synthetic detergents from mineral oil would await the harnessing of methods and technologies devised originally in the petroleum industry. By the late 1930s, immediately preceding World War II, synthetic detergents based on nonfatty raw materials were just beginning to appear in small quantities. The changeover from fatty to non-fatty raw materials was greatly accelerated through the adoption of techniques developed during the war.[31]

The petroleum industry's knowledge of the cracking process was applied in the detergent industry to specially selected petroleum waxes, from which long-chain alpha-olefins were obtained. These were then used for the manufacture of what would become one of the most important classes of synthetic detergents, the higher secondary alkyl sulfates. The technique of alkylation used in their manufacture had been developed within the petroleum industry for the production of high-octane aviation fuel.[32] During the war large alkylation plants were constructed in the United States for the production of aviation fuel, and after the war these plants became available for the manufacture of alkylate for the detergent industry.

The alkyl aryl sulfonates provided the postwar breakthrough for the large-

scale replacement of soap as the basis of household detergents. The first product of this type to be sold in the United States was an alkyl toluene sulfonate.[33] This, however, yielded washing powders that caked readily. Alkyl
benzene sulfonate (ABS), based either on propylene tetramer or tributylene,
did not have this drawback, and demand for this type of active matter grew
at a remarkable rate.[34] During the period 1943–48, the production of alkyl
benzene sulfonate tripled from twenty-five million to seventy-five million
pounds. The alkyl benzene sulfonate made from tetrapropylene proved to be
an outstanding surfactant, and during the period 1950–65 considerably more
than half the detergents used worldwide would be based on it.[35]

Alkyl benzene sulfonates possessed excellent washing abilities under all
conditions of use. For the first time, low cost all-purpose synthetic detergents
could be produced at a price competitive with soap. Their desirable properties
were confirmed "when a household package was introduced to the American
housewife and was readily accepted."[36] The fatty oil and alcohol based synthetic detergents that were already established, especially in midwestern hard
water areas, were subsequently reformulated to include alkyl benzene sulfonates. These events were part of the revolution that occurred in the detergent
industry in the decade following World War II. In the pre-war years, synthetic
detergents had been manufactured on a small scale, by relatively costly processes, from fatty oil and alcohol sources. Their use was confined largely to
the textile and leather industries and, with domestic use, to hard water areas.
Following the war, synthetic detergents were manufactured on a hitherto unprecedented scale by completely new methods, from non-fatty raw materials,
and came into widespread domestic use.[37]

In 1953, for the first time, more synthetic detergent than soap by weight
was sold; and by 1958 synthetic detergents constituted 72 percent of all detergents produced, including soap, and comprised more than 90 percent of
the detergents in household packaged cleaning products. By 1948 there had
already been some five hundred different synthetic detergent products on the
market. However, it was estimated that a relatively few nationally advertised
brands controlled 90 percent or more of retail sales.[38] These included, with
manufacturer and year of appearance on the market in parentheses, Swerl
(National Aniline, 1945); Tide (Procter and Gamble, 1946); Breeze (Lever
Brothers, 1947); Surf (Lever Brothers, 1948); and Fab (Colgate-Palmolive-
Peet, 1948). Swerl and Breeze belonged to the class of light-duty products
designed for dishwashing and laundering fine fabrics; Tide, Fab, and Surf
belonged to the class of heavy-duty detergents containing "builders."

As noted, "builders" are various chemical compounds that are mixed with
surfactants to increase the surfactants' cleaning effectiveness. The most common builders in the mid-1950s included complex phosphates, sodium sulfate,

carboxymethyl cellulose, silicates, and sodium carbonate. One commercial synthetic detergent of that time, for example, was 30 percent alkyl benzene sulfonate, 28 percent polyphosphate, 6 percent sodium silicate, 35 percent sodium sulfate, and 1 percent carboxymethyl cellulose.[39] The diagram in figure 1 offers a general comparison of the contents of typical contemporary packages of synthetic detergent and soap powder.

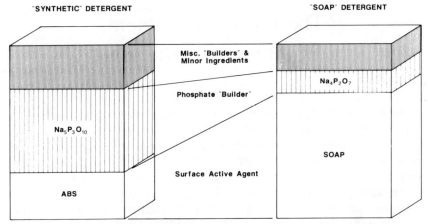

Figure 1. A representation of the two major types of packaged household washing products. From *Water Pollution Control*, Hearings before a Special Subcommittee on Air and Water Pollution of the Committee on Public Works, U.S. Senate, 88th Cong., 1st sess. (June 17, 18, 19, 20, 25, and 26, 1963, p. 632)

I will continue to use "synthetic detergent" in the sense understood by the general public: a cleaning agent other than soap. When the surface-active agent portion of the package is referred to, I will employ the industry's term, "surfactant." As will be seen, attention in subsequent chapters will focus on the surfactant in packaged synthetic detergents.

The rapid substitution of soap in many of its uses by synthetic detergents in the decades following World War II occurred not only in the United States but also in the United Kingdom and the Federal Republic of Germany. All three would quickly find that the new wonder cleaners created unanticipated environmental problems.

II

The Foaming Problem: Eruption and Analysis

Beginning in late 1947, sewage treatment plant operators throughout the United States reported unprecedented foaming at their plants. At the same time, foam began to pollute rivers and lakes, some of which served as sources of domestic water supply. Sewage treatment and water purification treatment officials pointed to the new synthetic detergents as the cause of the foaming, but the detergent industry disagreed. The question of the relationship between detergents and foaming became the "hottest" research topic in the field of sanitary engineering during the 1950s.[1] By 1958 Clair N. Sawyer, professor of sanitary chemistry at MIT, had decisively examined the question and identified the specific surfactants causing the foaming.

Throughout soap's history, the disposal of domestic and industrial soapy wastes had caused no serious environmental problems.[2] In the mid-twentieth century, soap caused no difficulties for the sewage treatment plants that had been built to serve urban communities from the late nineteenth century.[3] The principal reason for soap's trouble-free behavior was that it was readily precipitated or removed as scum in settling tanks and receiving waters by naturally occurring calcium and magnesium ions.[4]

It seems that the possibility that synthetic detergents might cause environmental problems was not considered as they were being placed on the domestic market. Today we expect the potential "environmental impact" of a new product to be assessed before it is put to use, but that is because in regard to environmental consciousness we stand on the near side of a watershed, which the experience with the first generation of petroleum-based synthetic detergents helped create.

On an October day in 1947 an unidentified detergent manufacturer distributed free samples of a liquid "soapless soap" to homes in Mount Penn, Pennsylvania.[5] On the following day the supervisor of the local sewage treatment plant was shocked when he inspected his normally well behaved aeration tanks.[6] The sewage liquid, instead of being visible and seen to be ruffled by the action of diffused air as usual, was hidden under a huge blanket of billowing white suds from two to five feet thick. When contacted, the manufacturer made no effort to disown responsibility for the foam and offered prompt help. Company chemists subsequently concluded that in all probability the Mount Penn residents had used twice as much detergent as recommended, thereby causing an abnormal concentration of detergent in the sewage. The plant supervisor expressed the hope that Mount Penn housewives would in future exercise discretion when using synthetic detergents.

Manufacturers could direct their chemists to "build suds" into detergents or not. None were built into industrial detergents, because "suds serve a doubtful purpose, are bulky and get in the way, and actually interfere with cleaning actions, decreasing efficiency."[7] Many establishments, including bottle-cleaning plants and dairies, preferred detergents with no foaming properties at all. They had found that such sudless detergents removed dirt so thoroughly, and left equipment and containers so clean, that subsequent sterilization was often only a precautionary gesture. Suds were merely a nuisance. However, for generations the American housewife had been taught, frequently by manufacturers, to associate good cleaning with thick suds; and plentiful suds were built into detergents sold for domestic use.[8]

Throughout the late nineteen-forties, as domestic consumption of detergents increased rapidly, sewage plant operators increasingly reported problems with foaming. In August of 1949, for example, the aerators at the larger of the two Batavia, Illinois, treatment plants began a "violent frothing" that continued unabated throughout ensuing months.[9] The sudsy "supercharge," besides being bulky, sticky, smelly, and generally physically bothersome in the plant itself, was accompanied by a deterioration of both the plant effluent and the settling qualities of the aeration liquid. The Bartlesville, Oklahoma, activated-sludge plant was reported in March, 1950, to have had foam on it for so long that the plant superintendent had come to accept foam as part of normal operating conditions. "On a good day," the superintendent said, "the suds sail around in the air like little fluffy clouds."[10] With such occurrences multiplying, the Division of Water, Sewage, and Sanitation of the American Chemical Society held a symposium on the effects of detergents in water and sewage and in sanitation at the society's annual meeting in April, 1951.[11] One optimistic participant believed that the undesirable effects of detergents, including foaming and prevention of easy settling and filtration of solid material in sewage, might all be overcome without making radical changes in disposal treatment. But the problem would prove more difficult to solve than he imagined.

Some people were soon arguing that factors other than the presence of detergents were more important in producing excessive foam in sewage treatment plants. In early 1951 a plant in San Antonio, Texas, developed foam about eight feet high. In investigating this occurrence, W. N. Wells and C. H. Scherer, the plant's superintendent and chemist, respectively, had the cooperation of one detergent manufacturer, the Procter and Gamble Company. At that time, due to the many different types of detergents and their complex reactions and interactions with the varied contents of sewage liquor, it had not been possible to develop tests for determining the amount of detergent present in a given raw sewage. One qualitative test taught that if the pH of a sample of the liquor was reduced to 3.0, and the liquor well shaken, detergent was present if foam developed.[12] From their personal experience, and from comments in the literature, Wells and Scherer knew of the tendency of a liquor with a low, recycled solids content to produce foam; on the other hand, they also knew the value of a high solids content in preventing foam formation. So they investigated the relationship between solids content and foaming under the conditions encountered in the San Antonio plant. They varied the concentration of the solids and noted the associated foaming tendency. Wells and Scherer found that a solids level of about fourteen hundred ppm was sufficiently high to prevent frothing. Furthermore, they found that at this level the direct addition of the synthetic detergent Tide (twenty-eight hundreds pounds of which had been supplied by the Procter and Gamble Company) to an aeration tank, even at extremely high concentrations, did not cause any objectionable foaming.[13] Even under conditions of low solids, when foaming was likely to occur, the addition of detergent did not seem to increase foaming.

An editorial in the issue of *Sewage and Industrial Wastes* in which these results were reported commented that while Wells and Scherer had proved fairly conclusively that foam formation was not likely to be troublesome in the presence of high concentrations of anionic[14] detergents if sixteen hundred ppm (Wells and Scherer actually found fourteen hundred ppm) or more of suspended solids were carried in the mixed liquor, nevertheless, this knowledge would bring no solace to plant operators who had to operate at lower mixed liquor solids levels.[15] The editorial also argued that the San Antonio results did "not 'whitewash' synthetic detergents as the cause of aeration tank suds"—many activated sludge plants had operated with low mixed liquor solids prior to 1940 without the voluminous foam that was now frequently encountered.

However, W. R. Gowdy, of Procter and Gamble's chemical division in Cincinnati, in a paper on the chemical structure and action of synthetic detergents presented at the annual meeting of the Ohio Sewage and Industrial Wastes Treatment Conference in May, 1952, concluded that the facts he had reported indicated that "the extremely dilute concentrations of synthetics found in sewage [could] hardly alone be capable of causing frothing or settling problems."[16] His conclusion, he added, was supported by the results of Wells and Scherer's full-scale tests.

Some six months later Gowdy participated in a symposium on detergents at the annual meeting of the Federation of Sewage and Industrial Wastes Association. He revealed the industry's attitude in remarking that "in some quarters . . . speculation on the possible relationship between frothing and detergents has taken on the reputation of a fact, so often has it been repeated." Gowdy explained that as it seemed inconceivable that such "high dilutions" of detergents as those found in domestic sewage could make suds in such dirty water, an obvious starting point was to try to create froth deliberately in the activated sludge process by adding detergents in amounts well above what might ever be found in sewage, even with a greatly increased use of detergents. He again noted the results of Wells and Scherer, adding that it had seemed worthwhile to repeat their tests in a different type of plant to determine whether similar principles held. As there were many relatively small, mechanically aerated, activated sludge plants in use around the country, Procter and Gamble researchers had decided to experiment on a typical one in Bryan, Ohio. Results obtained were similar to those of Wells and Scherer. The researchers also collected case histories for ten other plants, most of which were experiencing or had experienced foaming problems. In all cases of serious foaming the plants were found to be carrying relatively low solids. Also, plants that normally did not have foaming problems experienced similar troubles when they carried solids at low levels. Gowdy concluded that "it does not appear that commonly sold household detergents play any important part in practical frothing problems encountered in the treatment of sewage by the activated sludge process."[17]

At the same symposium two other industry spokesmen—Lawrence Flett and Lester F. Hoyt, director and manager, respectively, of detergent application research, new products division, Allied Chemical and Dye Corporation—presented a paper on the composition and behavior of detergents. They declared that "there is no established proof that sudsing, or in fact any other problem of the ordinary sewage treatment system, has been caused by anionic detergent."[18] They acknowledged that there had been "a very few isolated instances of difficulties" when "certain circumstances" had resulted in excessive amounts of detergents being introduced into small local sewers; but the circumstances had been so unusual that they were without general significance. During discussion of the Flett-Hoyt paper, Willem Rudolfs, a Rutgers University professor studying the effects of detergents on water treatment plants, countered that although it was probably true that no one had been able to connect foaming at sewage plants directly with detergents, there seemed to be considerable circumstantial evidence that foaming had become more pronounced with the increased use of detergents. Another discussant, a consulting engineer, added that there had been foaming at the Nassau County plant on Long Island with as much as two thousand ppm of suspended solids in the sewage liquor.[19]

Even granting that detergents caused foaming in sewage treatment plants, plant operators did not regard the occurrence of foam as too serious a problem. It could be solved simply, either by spraying water to beat down the foam or by using anti-foaming compounds. A much more serious problem, however, was the presence of detergents in domestic water supplies. In May, 1949, the American Water Works Association had held a panel discussion at its annual meeting on the effects of pollution by synthetic detergents.[20] It was not until four years later that the association formed a task group to study the problem. Then in early 1954 the institutional study of the effects of detergents was widened when the Ohio River Valley Water Sanitation Commission (ORSANCO) created a detergent subcommittee within its chemical industry committee to investigate the detergent "situation."[21]

The ORSANCO action followed up on the dismaying occurrences of foam at water purification plants all along the upper Ohio River, in particular at Wheeling, West Virginia, in the fall of 1953. As the superintendent of water purification at Wheeling reported: "It all started the last few days in November when the countryside received the first rain since the middle of July. The creeks which had been dry or practically so all summer started to flow and the first indication of trouble was the day before Thanksgiving when a fishy odor was detected in the water. By November 30, and on December 1, this fish odor had developed into a 'decomposed whale odor' and if this was not enough there was froth and foam everywhere."[22] The foam rose to a level over four feet high on the raw water basin and two feet deep on the walks leading to the basin. On the Ohio River immediately below Dam No. 1, situated a mile downstream from the Wheeling purification plant, a blanket of foam from eleven to twenty-four inches thick extended across the seven-hundred-foot width of the river. The foam spread two hundred feet downstream from the dam on one side and more than a mile on the other. Analysis of the foam showed it to be "almost pure synthetic detergent." The superintendent was unable to say whether or not the purification process removed detergents; and if not, what effects detergents might have on persons ingesting them.

There were sound reasons then for paying increased attention to the relation of detergents to foaming in sewage treatment and water purification plants.[23] The most systematic and incisive study of that relationship in the United States was conducted by Clair N. Sawyer, professor of sanitary chemistry at MIT, in collaboration with several research assistants. Sawyer's investigations were conducted on his own initiative and were supported financially by the National Institutes of Health and the U.S. Public Health Service.

One of the first things Sawyer did was to study, with William O. Lynch, the foaming tendency of various detergents. Their simple apparatus consisted of an upright lucite pipe, nine feet high and four inches in internal diameter, having a small, porous, air-diffusion bulb inserted near the closed bottom.[24] The column was filled with a 50-ppm detergent solution to a depth of six and a half feet above the diffuser, and air was passed through. The eleven detergents tested were bought on the retail market and solutions were made using the local (Cambridge, Mass.) tap water. A marked difference was found in the foaming characteristics of the various detergents. In view of the fact that Dreft, Tide, and Surf were all classed as anionic detergents, a group known for its copious suds, Sawyer and Lynch were surprised to find an extreme contrast between Tide on the one hand, and Dreft and Surf on the other. Tide foamed rather early in the run to create a one-inch head of weak foam, and it maintained this level throughout the run; but Dreft and Surf each continued to pile up a deeper and deeper head of rich foam throughout the aeration period. Of the other anionics studied, Vel, Breeze, and Cheer were similar to Dreft and Surf; Oxydol was similar to Tide; and Fab fell between the two extremes. In the nonionic class Glim and Joy were found to be rich foamers, whereas All showed no foaming tendency whatever. These findings contradicted the accepted view of anionics as high foamers and nonionics as low foamers.

The findings were also important in that they challenged the industry's defense of detergents by revealing how misleading it was to take the foaming tendencies of detergents in washing machines or dishpans as indices of their foaming actions under differing conditions, especially under different temperatures. As Sawyer and Lynch commented, to anyone who had observed Tide's rich suds in hot dishpan water or All's "controlled sudsing" in an automatic washer's even hotter water, their respective poor- and non-foaming characteristics when used under the conditions of the investigation seemed "quite noteworthy."[25] Sawyer and Lynch suggested that their findings might explain why the plant-scale tests of foaming in the diffused-air activated sludge plant at San Antonio had led Gowdy to state that commonly sold household detergents did not appear to be an important cause in practical foaming problems. The detergent used in the San Antonio tests had been, we recall, Tide.

Sawyer and Lynch concluded that "synthetic detergents vary markedly in their ability to suds, from severe frothing to no frothing at all, hence neither blanket condemnation nor blanket exoneration of their role in frothing difficulties at sewage treatment plants seems justified."[26] They added that those detergents which foamed and were at the same time resistant to biological degradation were capable of causing foam in receiving waters, especially if those waters were relatively clean.

The question of the biological degradation of detergents was one that had been considered by others before it was addressed by Sawyer and a second collaborator, Richard H. Bogan. Together they investigated the biochemical degradation of the principal surfactants used in compounding detergents. In all, thirty-six surfactants were obtained in the purest possible form from the principal manufacturers and examined both under conditions representative of biological sewage treatment practice and conditions simulating the natural biological purification processes of receiving waters.

Biological utilization of organic materials generally involves use of oxygen, production of carbon dioxide, and multiplication or growth of microorganisms availing themselves of the energy in the materials. Under aerobic conditions the extent and speed of the changes occurring can best be followed by measuring the oxygen utilized. Two techniques are commonly used: the standard five-day biochemical oxygen demand (BOD) test, and manometric techniques involving use of equipment such as the Warburg respirometer.[27] The procedure employed by Bogan and Sawyer was to follow the biological oxidation of the detergents by means of both the Warburg apparatus and the BOD technique. An acclimated activated sludge and domestic sewage were used as seed in the BOD determinations.[28]

The results obtained by Bogan and Sawyer indicated that certain surfactants appeared to serve readily as bacterial food and, consequently, were subject to rapid biological stabilization.[29] The remaining surfactants were at least partially available as bacterial food and, hence, were subject to a slight to moderate degree of biological degradation.[30] Members of the first group were not likely to cause foaming problems in sewage treatment plants or receiving waters, but the opposite was true of members of the second group, which, moreover, were being more and more widely used. Sawyer and Bogan concluded that there was an immediate need for fundamental knowledge of the biochemical behavior of the principal surfactants. From their observations of the behavior of the alkyl aryl sulfonates—"Generically, there is no basis for differentiating the alkylbenzene sulfonates of commerce and yet biochemically, so to speak, a marked difference does exist"—they hypothesized that the biochemical degradation of surfactants was a function of their chemical constitution and could be strongly influenced by seemingly small changes in the nature of certain molecular components.[31]

Sawyer and Bogan proceeded to study the relationship between a surfactant's molecular structure and its susceptibility to biochemical oxidation. The method employed was as before.[32] The aerobic assimilation of a number of organic substances, representing both the major commercial surfactants as well as certain of their molecular constituents, was studied. Only materials of the highest possible degree of purity or of known chemical definition were selected.

Among the surfactants studied were three alkyl benzene sulfonates: n-dodecylbenzene sulfonate, kerylbenzene sulfonate, and tetrapropylene benzene sulfonate.[33] The first was obtained from the Atlantic Refining Company and was a pure chemical identity. The other two were supplied by the Procter and Gamble Company and represented middle portions of a narrow distillation cut taken from each of two reasonably well defined commercial preparations. The results suggested that the biochemical oxidation of the alkyl benzene sulfonates was strongly influenced by the nature of the alkyl group. The behavior of n-dodecylbenzene sodium sulfonate showed that this type of organic compound was "not inherently resistant" to biological assimilation. The kerylbenzene sulfonate investigated was representative of one of the two major alkyl benzene sulfonates of commerce. This material was characterized by alkyl groups that were essentially straight-chain hydrocarbons and was structurally somewhat similar to n-dodecylbenzene sulfonate. It was found to be slightly more resistant to biochemical stabilization than was the latter. The tetrapropylene benzene sulfonate represented the principal alkyl aryl sulfonate of commerce. It was a complex, isomeric mixture in which the alkyl groups were highly branched polymers of four propane molecules. In marked contrast to the first two alkyl benzene sulfonates, tetrapropylene benzene sulfonate was strongly resistant to biochemical oxidation. Such resistance thus appeared to be the result of a highly branched alkyl group. A British investigator, C. Hammerton, published a similar finding the following month. He found that "if the alkyl group has a straight chain, the compound is susceptible to biochemical oxidation, but if the alkyl group is branched, then bacterial degradation will either be delayed or substantially resisted according to the degree of branching. Highly or multi-branched alkyl groups appear to confer great stability upon the detergent molecule."[34]

Sawyer and Bogan decided that experimental investigation of substances resembling the alkyl group would shed light on the role it played in controlling the biochemical oxidation of alkyl benzene sulfonate. But first they studied sodium benzene sulfonate and found it to be markedly more susceptible to biochemical oxidation than benzene.[35] They concluded that apparently the presence of the sulfonate group materially altered the behavior of the benzene ring. However, such bio-oxidative activation was not observed with molecules in which 2-, 3-, and 4-carbon-atom side chains were linked to the benzene sulfonate group. The biochemical oxidation of the alkyl benzene type of molecule appeared to be related to the nature of the alkyl group. The even-numbered ethyl and n-butyl alkyl groups were apparently more susceptible to oxidation than either the odd-numbered n-propyl or the highly branched tertiary-butyl alkyl groups. The results tended to confirm the importance of branching of an alkyl group in restricting oxidation of the alkyl benzene molecule.

The most commonly used alkyl groups were derived largely from two sources—fatty acids and petroleum hydrocarbons, both paraffins and olefins.[36] The spatial configuration of the alkyl carbon chain, which could contain from eight to twenty or more carbon atoms, could be straight or highly branched. Best detergency appeared to be associated with those surfactants in which the alkyl carbon chains contained on the average twelve carbon atoms. The biochemical significance of branching in an alkyl group appeared to be primarily a chemical phenomenon. Among organic chemists it was understood that replacement of an active hydrogen with CH_3, or other alkyl group or halogen, often altered the chemical reactivity of the molecule either by blocking chemically reactive positions or by activating other positions. So Sawyer and Bogan suggested that the substitution of methyl and possibly other alkyl groups for hydrogen in a hydrocarbon chain might very effectively block or retard oxidative degradation of that chain.

The joint studies of Sawyer and his colleagues had shown that certain surfactants could produce copious foam and at the same time resist biodegradation. Such surfactants could therefore pass undegraded through sewage treatment plants and continue to produce foam in receiving waters. In collaboration with another of Sawyer's research assistants, James R. Simpson, Sawyer and Bogan next studied the lifespans of surfactants in natural river waters under controlled conditions in the laboratory.[37] They used water from the local Charles and Ipswich rivers, both of which were assumed to be natural habitats for organisms capable of degrading surfactants. The particular surfactants studied were n-dodecyl sulfate—representing what were now described for the first time as "biologically soft" materials—and keryl and tetrapropylene benzene sulfonates, representing materials with "considerable resistance to biological attack"—soon to be commonly referred to as "biologically hard." Tetrapropylene benzene sulfonate was specifically included because it represented the major surfactant used in compounding retail anionic detergents at the time.

Each surfactant was added both to river water and to river water mixed with synthetic sewage. In the first instance a condition was established similar to that encountered in waters receiving effluent from a complete sewage treatment plant; and in the second, a condition similar to that in waters receiving effluent from a primary treatment plant. Synthetic sewage was used rather than domestic, as the latter would have contained unknown amounts of surfactants. The mixtures were mechanically stirred to simulate the turbulent conditions of a river. No attempt was made to control the temperature, which ranged from twenty-one to twenty-seven degrees centigrade, corresponding to summer conditions. Samples were taken for analysis at four- to six-hour intervals from the mixtures containing alkyl sulfate and at two-day intervals from those containing keryl and tetrapropylene benzene sulfonates.

The results agreed well with what Sawyer, Bogan, and Simpson had anticipated from their knowledge of five-day BOD and Warburg respirometric studies. Alkyl sulfates disappeared quite rapidly, their lifespan under summer conditions appearing to be of the order of one day. However, both keryl and tetrapropylene benzene sulfonate, and especially the latter, disappeared only very slowly. Even after some twenty days significant amounts of residual surfactant persisted. Keryl and tetrapropylene benzene sulfonates appeared to have half-lives of about seven and sixteen days, respectively. The latter, the most important commercial surfactant, was characterized by Sawyer, Bogan, and Simpson as "extremely resistant to oxidation." In their published findings the investigators made the following illuminating observation:

> Man's knowledge concerning the biochemical degradation of organic materials has been largely limited to that of fats, carbohydrates, and proteins simply because they represent the major foods of man and, therefore, predominate in the wastes which he creates. The evolution of the age of synthetic chemistry has brought with it many new compounds and products which have little relation to man's food supply but rather are articles of commerce which are of great importance in modern-day living. Many of these substances have no counterpart in naturally occurring materials so it is not surprising to find that bacteria or enzyme systems do not exist which will accomplish their rapid degradation. In view of the fact that lignin has, undoubtedly, been present in nature ever since life began on earth and, yet, no enzyme systems have been evolved for its rapid degradation, it would seem that evolutionary processes cannot be counted on to come to our immediate rescue.[38]

Sawyer and his collaborators had now established that the most widely used surfactant, tetrapropylene benzene sulfonate, was also the most resistant to biodegradation. Consequently, it had the potential to cause foam both in sewage treatment plants and in receiving waters; but did it? What were the relationships between biological degradation, or the lack of it, and the occurrence of foam? Some believed that detergents were incapable of foaming in the dilute concentrations commonly encountered in sewage. However, as mentioned above, Lynch and Sawyer had largely dispelled this idea in their study of the behavior of dilute concentrations of commercially packaged detergents in tap water. Nevertheless, the question still remained unanswered as to how low concentrations of synthetic detergents behaved in sewage, or more particularly, in the presence of activated sludge. Sawyer and Bogan set out to answer the question. They studied the frothing behavior of nine different surfactants, including tetrapropylene benzene sulfonate, in the presence of activated sludge. These nine were representative of approximately 85–90 percent of the surfactants encountered in domestic sewage. The results relating to foam persistence are summarized in the following table.[39]

Frothing Behavior of Activated Sludge* Containing 50 Mg. per Liter of Various Syndets

| | Degree of Frothing | | | |
| | Contact Time | | | |
Syndet	5 min.	6 hr.	21 hr.	120 hr.
Anionic				
Alkyl Benzene Sulfonates:				
Straight chain type n-dodecyl	very slight	nil	———	———
Keryl	severe	severe	moderate	slight
Branched chain type propene tetramer	severe	severe	severe	severe
Alkyl sulfate n-dodecyl	slight	nil	———	———
Sulfonated amide sodium-N-methyl-N-oleoyl taurate	strong	nil	———	———
Sulfonated esters derivative of ethyl oleate	nil	———	———	———
Nonionic				
Alkyl phenoxy polyethoxy-ethanol type	severe	moderate	moderate	moderate
Polyexyethylene fatty acid amide	slight	slight	slight	nil
Polyoxyethylene fatty acid ester	slight	slight	nil	

*Activated sludge systems contained 1,200 mg. per liter of aeration solids except in the case of the three acyclic sulfonate systems which contained 1,000 mg. per liter of solids.

The three nonionic surfactants produced a rich close-textured foam, contrary to the general view that this type of detergent did not foam. Among the alkyl benzene sulfonates, Sawyer and Bogan found that the branched-chain propylene tetramer alkyl group was associated with the heaviest foaming. A straight-chain structure appeared to be less conducive to frothing, other things being equal. Thus Bogan and Sawyer concluded that small amounts of some important surfactants were capable of inducing excessive foaming in aerated activated sludge.

In a related study Sawyer and Devere W. Ryckman reported that the propylene benzene sulfonates (and all tertiary benzene sulfonates) could be expected to survive for great distances in rivers. This agreed with the findings of Sawyer, Bogan, and Simpson, previously mentioned, and of Hammerton, who had found a half-life of about fifteen days under simulated river conditions.[40] Sawyer and Ryckman's experiments with activated sludge demonstrated that even the most potent treatment process was not effective in completing the destruction of tertiary benzene sulfonates. Trickling filters would have been even less effective. They concluded that "the tertiary benzene sulfonates constituted the greatest threat to public water supplies of any of the anionic type detergents." As over 80 percent of all surfactants sold were of this type, it was "also quite evident that the tertiary alkyl benzene sulfonates deserve[d] special attention."[41]

In October, 1957, at the annual meeting of the Federation of Sewage and Industrial Wastes Associations, Sawyer gave an appraisal of current knowledge of the foaming problem in relation to detergents, based mainly on the studies directed by him at MIT during the preceding five years. He offered a composite interpretation of why foaming was not a problem in raw sewage, but gradually became so as aeration of activated sludge mixtures progressed, as shown in figure 2.[42] Sawyer said that in regard to foam, sewage consisted of three types of materials—anti-foams, foam-producing substances, and neutral substances. In raw or settled sewage the anti-foaming substances were normally present in sufficient amounts to prevent foaming. As biological degradation of the sewage occurred, all components of the sewage except the biologically hard detergents readily stabilized. Thus, as the concentration of the anti-foaming materials decreased, foaming developed in intensity depending upon the amount of biologically hard surfactant contained in the sewage.

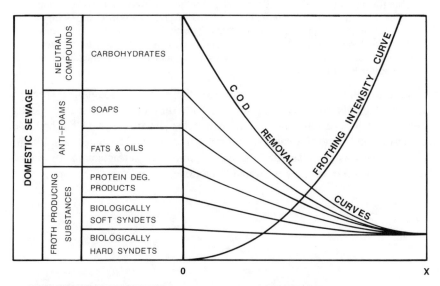

SEWAGE CHARACTERISTICS   AERATION TIME

Figure 2. Character of domestic sewage and relation of frothing character during activated sludge treatment to biological assimilability.

Basically, the magnitude of the foaming problem would be related to the rate at which the anti-foaming materials were destroyed, the concentration of residual surfactants (such as ABS), the depth of the aeration tanks, and the rate of air application.

Control of frothing in activated sludge plants had been accomplished in many cases by maintaining a high concentration of aeration solids. But this practice had not always been successful, and had become less so in recent years as the synthetic detergent concentration had increased. The experience of the plant in Cranston, Rhode Island, illustrates the point. In 1952 it had been reported that foaming could be controlled by maintaining aeration solids above two thousand ppm; but by 1956 foaming had become so severe at Cranston that a spray system had to be installed. Sawyer thought it was unreasonable to expect the adsorptive ability of activated sludge to keep pace with the increased concentration of synthetic detergents in sewage, meaning more and more plants would be forced into installing foam control facilities. However, there could be an alternative future:

> It is reasonable to assume that syndets are here to stay and their popularity, though not necessarily so, is apt to increase. It becomes the responsibility of those in the business of sewage treatment to focus attention on untoward effects which such materials produce and call the attention of the manufacturers to the problems. But the claims must be positive and the pitfalls of blanket statements must be avoided. With a basis of mutual trust, it would seem reasonable that manufacturers of syndets will attempt to modify their products so as to minimize problems related thereto. On the basis of present knowledge, it appears reasonable to urge producers of syndets to substitute biologically "soft" surfactants for biologically "hard" materials as much as possible and to initiate research to discover new and perhaps better biologically "soft" surfactants which can compete with ABS.[43]

Here was sound advice. The question of the causes of foaming in sewage treatment plants and receiving streams had from 1952 been systematically studied by Sawyer and his various research assistants at MIT.[44] They had come to understand the causes, and consequently could suggest a solution. From at least as early as 1957 the manufacturers of surfactants and the producers of detergents knew what had to be done.

III

The Industry's Response
to the Detergent Pollution Problem

Although the detergent industry continued to deny that the foaming problem was caused by detergents (and it would not say otherwise until a solution was at hand), at the same time it initiated its own studies. The initial phase of the industry's research program dealt primarily with the fate of surfactants in sewage treatment plants, and the second phase dealt with the potentially much more serious problem of the contamination of groundwater by surfactants. The industry concluded that although the leading surfactant, alkyl benzene sulfonate (ABS), was not completely degraded in sewage works or cesspools, in the concentrations in which it was found in surface and groundwaters it did not constitute a threat to human health. Nevertheless, the industry knew that the public would not tolerate pollution by ABS.

During late 1953, highly unusual frothing erupted on the Ohio River at Wheeling, West Virginia. Troubled by this occurrence, Edward J. Cleary, executive director and chief engineer of the Ohio River Valley Water Sanitation Commission (ORSANCO), recommended that a new subcommittee be created within the Commission's Chemical Industry Committee to investigate pollution by detergents.[1] ORSANCO's role was to coordinate and supplement the activities of eight states (Illinois, Indiana, Kentucky, New York, Ohio, Pennsylvania, Virginia, and West Virginia) that had undertaken to cooperate "in the control of future pollution and the abatement of existing pollution" in the Ohio River.[2] On February 11, 1954, the Detergent Subcommittee was formed.

The new committee's first undertaking was developing a means of analyzing for detergents. Until reliable methods were available for measuring the trace amounts of detergents "likely" to be found in tap water, river water, and sewage, all investigations of the effects of detergents obviously would be seriously handicapped. Work was begun initially on methods of analysis for

ABS, as this material was the most common of the surface-active agents in the packaged synthetic detergents sold on the domestic market.[3]

The subcommittee soon informed the Association of American Soap and Glycerine Producers (AASGP) of its work and invited manufacturers both of detergent raw materials and finished detergent products to cooperate with it in developing reliable analytical methods. Various companies responded, including Atlantic Refining, California Research Corporation, Colgate-Palmolive, Continental Oil, Lever Brothers, Monsanto, National Aniline, and Procter and Gamble. These companies, all members of the AASGP, soon formed an official committee of their own, the Analytical Subcommittee, to develop analytical methods.[4]

When these various efforts began, a colorimetric test for ABS using methylene blue dye was widely used. The dye and ABS are both soluble in water, but insoluble in chloroform. However, ABS reacts with methylene blue to form a complex that is soluble in chloroform. The intensity of color produced in chloroform by the complex can be measured photometrically and compared with a calibration curve drawn up using measured amounts of ABS.[5] The initial work of the AASGP Analytical Subcommittee, as well as a task group that had been created in September, 1953, by the American Water Works Association (AWWA) to study the effects of synthetic detergents on water supplies, was to standardize the method, providing a scale for measuring from 0.025 to 100 ppm of ABS.[6] The method was found to be unsatisfactory, however. Various solutions, including urine, tea, coffee, and distilled water extracts of such materials as straw, leaves, and rotted wood, appeared by this method to contain ABS when, in fact, they did not.[7] The AWWA task group stressed that as the natural production of surface-active agents is considerable, raw waters should be expected to contain a variety of natural surfactants.

Various individuals and groups attempted to overcome the shortcomings of the methylene blue test. One procedure, which would be adopted as the official British method, was based on methylene blue but had the chloroform extraction performed under alkaline instead of acidic conditions. A second procedure employed the same basic principles but employed methyl green as the dye and extracted into benzene instead of chloroform. A yet more precise, although more complicated, procedure employed a combination of ABS extraction with methylheptylamine followed by further extraction with methylene blue.[8]

By 1956 the AASGP's Analytical Subcommittee had developed the referee, or infrared, method as a specific, quantitative procedure that provided an unequivocal identification and measure of ABS in water or sewage.[9] Although not complicated, this method required time, infrared equipment, and, when analyzing water, a large sample whose size depended upon the level of

ABS present—for example, if ABS were present at about 1 ppm, at least a 10-liter sample was required. For these reasons, the method would not be used routinely, but only when an accurate determination was called for. Even when analyzing sewage samples, which because of their higher concentrations of ABS could be smaller than water samples, the infrared method was used primarily as a referee procedure when the ABS level was required to be known with greater precision than was possible with other methods.[10]

In the referee method the water or sewage sample was passed through a column filled with a selected analytical-grade activated carbon that adsorbed the ABS, thus separating it from many "interferences" and concentrating it. The ABS and any interferences that had been adsorbed simultaneously were then desorbed from the carbon, and the mixture was subjected to several purification steps to remove the interferences present. The final step was a methylheptylamine extraction into chloroform. The amine complex was then examined using an infrared spectrophotometer. By comparison with known standards, the amount of ABS present could be determined.[11]

When in early 1955 it appeared that satisfactory analytical techniques would be developed, ORSANCO's Detergent Subcommittee appealed once more to the AASGP to support research on the possible effects of synthetic detergents both in water supplies and in water and sewage treatment plants.[12] During the previous year the AASGP had already initiated a research program to "(a) determine whether any of the reported problems [at sewage treatment and water purification plants] really did concern detergents, and (b) help in correcting any problems if it developed that detergents were actually involved."[13] This program had been initiated by, and would be directed largely by, the Research Steering Committee of the Association's Technical Advisory Council. In 1960 the committee was composed of representatives of ten companies: Monsanto Chemical, Lever Brothers, Atlantic Refining, Calgon, California Research Corporation, Colgate-Palmolive, Continental Oil, Victor Chemical Works, Westvaco Mineral Products Division, and Procter and Gamble. The association's method of operation was to have the research steering committee recommend which projects should be carried out by outside groups, which project should go to which group, and the extent to which each project should be funded.[14] The committee's recommendations required the approval of the Technical Advisory Council and the association's Board of Directors before funds could be appropriated. Such funds were solicited from all member companies of the association and occasionally from interested nonmembers.

Whether responding in part to ORSANCO's request or, what is more likely, acting in its own self-interest, the association sponsored several studies involving ABS[15] in prominent university departments of sanitary engineering.

The association would eventually spend some \$300,000 on the projects.[16] It knew that in ABS the industry had an outstanding and inexpensive surfactant that it would not readily give up. But the association also knew that opposition to the foaming problems caused by ABS would likely increase. The crucial question became whether these problems could be overcome, or at least alleviated.

The first project sponsored by the research steering committee was carried out at MIT. Earlier, employees of Continental Oil, a company represented on the research steering committee, had discussed with MIT engineers the biochemical degradation of surfactants in relation to the detergent pollution problem. The Continental Oil representatives had surmised that breakdown of a surfactant to the point where its surface activity was destroyed would probably remove it as a cause of foaming in sewage, and would completely eliminate the problems in water treatment associated with detergents.[17] Now the association contracted with Ross E. McKinney, an associate professor of sanitary engineering at MIT, to study detergent degradation, which he would do from March, 1955, through June, 1958.

In collaboration with his colleague James M. Symons, an assistant professor of sanitary engineering, McKinney set out to investigate the fundamental microbiology of ABS metabolism. They began with the premise that if the structure of tetrapropylenebenzene sulfonate was as shown below, bacteria should exist that could degrade the molecule completely.

$$
\begin{array}{cccc}
\text{H} & \text{H} & \text{H} & \text{H} \\
\text{HCH} & \text{HCH} & \text{HCH} & \text{HCH} \\
\text{H} \mid & \text{H} \mid & \text{H} \mid & \text{H} \mid \\
\end{array}
$$

HC–C–C–C–C–C–C–CH
H H H H H H H |

with the benzene ring attached:
HC=C–CH
HC=C–CH (ring) with SO$_3$Na

This molecular structure, they reasoned, might be regarded as having three components: tetrapropylene side-chain, benzene ring, and sulfonate group. Having researched the bacteriological literature they concluded that bacteria should be able to metabolize both the saturated hydrocarbon side chain and the benzene ring. Finding little about the behavior of the sulfonate group, they nevertheless concluded that it too could be metabolized. Their subsequent tests confirmed that indeed all three components could be metabolized by activated sludge. However, this result conflicted with their finding that ABS itself was not readily assimilated by the bacteria in activated sludge.

While struggling to understand this difference they happened to read a report issued by the Continental Oil Company indicating that analysis of Continental's alkylate showed it to be a mixture of many compounds; the average molecular structure of the ABS derived from it is shown below.[18]

```
            H    H    H
           HCH  HCH  HCH
    H  H  H  |   H  |   H   |   H
    HC—C—C—C—C—C—C—C—CH
    H  H  H  H  H  H  H  |   H
                         ⫶C⫶
                    HC        CH
                    HC        CH
                         C
                         |
                       SO₃Na
```

The key difference between this structure and that assumed by McKinney and Symons occurs at the junction of the hydrocarbon side-chain and the benzene ring, a quaternary carbon atom (one bonded to four other carbon atoms with single bonds) being present there. McKinney and Symons knew that the presence of a quaternary carbon would theoretically block bacterial metabolism at this point. They recalled that Sawyer and Ryckman had found that while both primary and secondary alkyl benzene sulfonates were degraded readily, the tertiary alkyl benzene sulfonates, those possessing a quaternary carbon, were not.[19]

The concept of a quaternary carbon block, according to McKinney and Symons, was based on the mechanism of hydrogen removal from organic matter. Inside sewage microorganisms, enzymes removed two hydrogen atoms at a time from adjacent carbon atoms on the surfactant molecule and oxidized them to water. With the quaternary carbon there was no hydrogen to be removed, so metabolism stopped at this point. The ABS fragment and the enzyme became bound together in a complex. Consequently, unless additional enzymes were made, even the partial metabolism would cease and free ABS would remain in solution. McKinney and Symons regarded the previously mentioned findings of Sawyer and Ryckman as confirmation of the soundness of the concept of quaternary block, news of which could only have been disappointing to the detergent industry.

Nevertheless, in spite of the fact that McKinney and Symons' work had primarily confirmed that ABS could not be completely degraded in sewage treatment plants, the industry seized upon secondary aspects of their work. They had shown that of thirty-five types of bacteria tested, seven showed good growth in a broth medium containing 1,000 mg/1 ABS, a high concentration by sewage plant standards, and seven (whether the same seven is unclear) were "definitely stimulated in the utilization of the synthetic sewage by the ABS."[20] One industry spokesman claimed that McKinney and Symons had established that ABS was not toxic to activated sludge bacteria—it would have been more accurate to say *all* activated sludge bacteria—that is, it did not impede the biological functioning of the plant.[21] This is a tale which grew with retelling. A year later W. K. Griesinger, chairman of the industry's Research Steering Committee, stated:

> One of the first questions we set out to answer was whether alkyl benzene sulfonate (ABS) is toxic to the bacteria that decomposes organic matter in sewage disposal plants. In a research program carried out at MIT, under the direction of Professor Ross McKinney, it was shown conclusively that ABS is not toxic to bacteria. They continue to decompose the organic matter present in sewage as effectively in the presence of ABS as they do in its absence. The misconception that ABS is harmful to bacteria still appears occasionally in print, but McKinney's work has generally been quite effective in clarifying this point.[22]

These were typical responses of the industry. Its spokesmen excelled in downplaying, and even denying, negative aspects of ABS's performance while at the same time stressing positive ones. Ironically, a year after Griesinger made his statement, his successor as chairman of the Research Steering Committee, J. David Justice, in lamenting difficulties being experienced by the committee in communicating what it regarded as the truth about detergents, said, "Another difficulty is the distortion of information, or lack of perspective through incorrect emphasis, without actually using incorrect information."[23]

If ABS was not completely degraded by activated sludge, to what degree was it degraded? This is the question that with the help of a research assistant, Eugene J. Donovan, McKinney next tackled. Assuming that the active ABS content in sewage reaching aeration tanks would not rise much above 10 mg/1 over the next few years, they set out to determine to what extent ABS could be metabolized by activated sludge when added at that concentration along with other organic nutrients. Five laboratory activated sludge units were set up, and analyses for ABS were made by the referee method.[24] ABS oxidation was found to range from 54 to 76 percent. However, it was impossible to determine whether the metabolized ABS had been completely, or only partially, metabolized. The degree of ABS removal appeared to be related to the rate of synthesis of sludge, and consequently to the quantity of sludge wasted. This indicated that high-rate or modified activated sludge systems could achieve the greatest ABS removals. However, even under the best of circumstances some 24 percent of the ABS would be undegraded.

In conventional activated sludge systems the concentration of organic matter was at a maximum immediately after its admission and a minimum at the end of the aeration period. The variations in organic concentration led to a feed-starve cycle, which prevented development of the optimum biological population. To overcome this deficiency, the complete-mixing activated sludge unit had been designed to permit a constant organic concentration and development of the optimum biological population. McKinney and Donovan found that using both domestic and synthetic sewage and an ABS concentration of 10 mg/l, approximately 60 percent reduction of ABS could be achieved with complete-mixing systems. With domestic sewage this rate was obtained when the suspended solids in the mixed liquor were about 3,000 mg/l. However, when the suspended solids were increased to 6,000 mg/l an 80 percent reduction of ABS was achieved.[25] Whether the ABS molecule had been completely, or only partially degraded, was, as before, impossible to determine. Once again McKinney's findings could not have been encouraging to the industry.

Nevertheless, as a result of them, and because conventional activated sludge systems could be converted to complete-mixing ones, a full-scale study was begun in Cranston, Rhode Island, under the joint-sponsorship of the AASGP and the state of Rhode Island.[26] The sewage plant at Cranston had two parallel conventional systems, one of which was converted to complete mixing, while the other served as a control. By 1960 the results obtained had not, however, fulfilled the promise of McKinney's laboratory findings.

Meanwhile, a second AASGP project had been placed with the sanitary engineering research laboratory at the University of California at Berkeley under P. H. McGauhey and Stephen A. Klein during the period May, 1955, through June, 1959. A second company represented on the AASGP Research Steering Committee, the California Research Corporation, had earlier seen the importance of investigating the fate of ABS in sewage treatment processes and had undertaken a full-scale study. Employing ABS tagged with radioactive sulphur, Ralph House and B. A. Fries had found that in the activated sludge plant used, some 80–90 percent of the ABS was destroyed in the normal treatment process.[27] These results were remarkably better than even the laboratory ones of McKinney and Donovan. But the AASGP must have had doubts about them, for it engaged McGauhey and Klein to follow up on this work and to make a more comprehensive study, under a wider range of conditions, of the fate of ABS in sewage treatment plants.[28] This research complemented that of McKinney and his coworkers.

Inasmuch as the initial step in sewage treatment is the separation of solids from liquids, McGauhey and Klein began by making determinations of the amount of ABS removed from sewage by primary sedimentation.[29] Previous work, based on colorimetric analysis, had indicated that some 30 percent of the ABS in raw sewage was adsorbed on solids settling out during a two-hour detention period. Initial determinations made by McGauhey and Klein using the methyl green method of analysis agreed with this figure. However, a great error inherent in the method was subsequently revealed by radioassay. The ABS used in this process was prepared by sulfonating small amounts of alkyl benzene with sulfur-35 in ordinary laboratory glassware. Radioassay determinations indicated that a value of a mere 2 percent was more typical for ABS removal by sedimentation.

Having established that primary sedimentation was of little significance in removing ABS, McGauhey and Klein turned to the study of secondary processes.[30] Because activated sludge was the most widely used secondary treatment process in large installations, and because foaming in aeration tanks had been blamed on detergents, the ability of activated sludge to degrade ABS, and the factors affecting that ability, became the principal concerns of their investigation. The results of their studies led McGauhey and Klein to conclude that activated sludge might be expected to remove an average of 50–60 percent of ABS when the latter's initial concentration was within the range encountered in raw sewage in the United States. This was somewhat below the average reported by McKinney and Donovan. Furthermore, studies of the effects of varying such factors as aeration rate, period of aeration, and solids concentration in the mixed liquor, within limits practical for activated sludge plants, failed to yield major increases in ABS removal, although increasing solids concentration produced a slight increase.

McGauhey and Klein, together with P. B. Palmer, next studied the ability of trickling filters to remove ABS from sewage. They employed a pilot-scale filter operating at various rates of recirculation.[31] Studies of operating trickling filters in Britain had indicated 39 percent removal in one installation and 58 percent in a second. But McGauhey's group found that only about 25 percent removal was attained under conditions that produced a high level of sewage treatment as indicated by BOD reduction. Thus trickling filters were about half as effective as activated sludge in removing ABS.

These various results suggested that the best that one could hope for was the removal of some 60 percent of the ABS content of sewage treated in an activated sludge plant. To achieve a higher percentage would require special removal procedures involving the modification of current practices or the introduction of intermediate or tertiary steps in the treatment of sewage. McGauhey's group studied such possibilities.

Efforts to enhance ABS removal by altering contemporary sewage treatment processes were confined largely to the activated sludge process, since it alone achieved normal values of appreciable magnitude.[32] Best results were obtained by maintaining high solids concentration (about 5,000 mg/1) where rapid sludge growth conditions were maintained. This measure, however, was found to boost the average ABS removal by only about 10 percent above the expected normal of 50 percent, while exhibiting the same wide fluctuation in daily removals characteristic of the normal plant.

Two activated sludge units in series were found to be no more effective than a single unit. Neither was a system in which the activated sludge carrying most of the quickly adsorbed unstable solids was diverted to a separate aeration tank after one hour in hopes of attenuating the organisms to the remaining high-ABS-low-BOD residue. From these and several other experiments McGauhey's group concluded that modification of the existing activated sludge process did not promise a means of achieving a high level of ABS removal.

They then turned to a consideration of special processes. Starting from the well-known fact that when frothing occurs the surface-active agent present is concentrated in the froth, McGauhey and Klein developed a process which they called "surface stripping." It involved two principal steps—inducing frothing by aeration, followed by removal and disposal of the induced froth. Intense aeration at a rate of about one cubic foot per gallon of sewage treated during a fifteen-minute or shorter period was found to concentrate, in the froth, more than 80 percent of the ABS in a 10 mg/1 solution. Whether applied to the primary or secondary sewage effluent, induced frothing was found to be equally effective, despite the fact that half of the ABS had already been removed from the secondary effluent by activated sludge. In either case a minimum residual of 1 mg/1 ABS was achieved, regardless of how much higher the concentration of ABS had originally been in the sewage frothed. In theory, surface stripping could have been utilized as either an intermediate or a tertiary process, but the practical problem of froth disposal dictated a tertiary process.

Concentration of ABS in froth was found to vary between 400 and 850 times that in the sewage treated, the wetter froths coming from primary sewage and the amount of entrained water being a function of a number of variables, including intensity of aeration. Under the best conditions an appreciable quantity of liquid—some three thousand gallons per million gallons of sewage treated—was associated with the separated froth. Evaporation of this liquid during total incineration was accomplished by extruding the froth into a burning chamber that used commercial gas as fuel. Partial incineration to reduce froth to a liquid residue also proved successful. However, in 1961 McGauhey and Klein were still seeking an economical means of disposing of froth.[33] Even if they had found one, the effluent from the tertiary treatment would still have contained ABS in the concentration of 1 mg/1. There seemed to be no way of preventing ABS from entering receiving waters. So once again an industry-sponsored research program had yielded little of comfort to the industry.

A third, related AASGP project, was conducted at the University of Wisconsin during 1955–59. L. P. Polkowski, G. A. Rohlich, and J. R. Simpson, respectively assistant professor, professor, and instructor in civil engineering, investigated both the causes and prevention of frothing in sewage treatment plants. This project followed up work by W. R. Gowdy that had shown reduced frothing in activated sludge plants when sludge solids were maintained at relatively high levels.[34] Gowdy had suggested that possibly frothing was not caused by detergents but by "something" that happened in the aeration tank itself. However, after a comprehensive study of frothing in activated sludge plants, Polkowski, Rohlich, and Simpson concluded that although low suspended solids concentration, protein degradation products, temperatures above 72°F, high pH values, and high aeration rates were all factors that contributed to foaming, nevertheless "the ABS concentration in the mixed liquor filtrates was significantly correlated to the frothing parameters and accounted for more of the variation than any other single factor." Once again, this was not good news for the industry. Prior to the study, the chairman of the AASGP's Research Steering Committee, F. J. Coughlin of Procter and Gamble, had commented that the Wisconsin research "project is, of course, of special interest to the association because synthetic detergents usually become headline material when frothing occurs."[35]

The research projects carried out at MIT, Berkeley, and Wisconsin all related to the behavior of ABS in sewage treatment plants. Taken together they showed that ABS was the principal source of foaming in the plants, and furthermore that up to 40 percent of all ABS would pass undegraded through the best contemporary plants into receiving waters. Worse yet, there seemed little prospect of finding an economic means of preventing ABS from entering those waters. On the other hand, none of the studies, and especially McKinney's, had shown ABS to affect adversely the operation of sewage plants, which were just as efficient with it as without it passing through. It was this aspect of the projects' findings that the industry chose to highlight.

It had of course been known, before these studies confirmed it, that detergents were entering receiving waters. Questions had been raised about the persistence of detergents in surface waters and their effects on treatment processes when these waters were used for domestic supplies. In a fourth project sponsored by the AASGP, James J. Morgan and Richard S. Englebrecht of the department of civil engineering at the University of Illinois surveyed phosphate and ABS concentrations in Illinois surface waters. Of interest here are their findings in regard to ABS.[36]

Their survey consisted of four parts, two of which will be considered. First, they examined water samples from seven lakes and reservoirs to determine ABS levels in water supplies free of significant domestic pollution. Next they sampled water at twenty-six locations on streams used as sources of water supply throughout the major Illinois river basins. These streams were believed to be receiving significant amounts of treated and untreated domestic wastes. The method of analytical determination for ABS was the standard methylene blue one. Morgan and Englebrecht were aware that, as with other dye methods, this one was subject to a variety of errors, which could be caused by either organic or inorganic compounds and take the form of negative as well as positive interferences. However, it had frequently been reported that in determining ABS in water, positive interferences were much more significant. Thus Morgan and Englebrecht assumed that the values they obtained were probably higher than the true values and referred to them as "apparent" ABS concentrations.

In the lakes and reservoirs sampled, apparent ABS values were found to be "low," ranging from zero to 0.016 ppm.[37] As almost no detergents were expected to find their way to these sources, the apparent ABS measured was taken to be the result of positive interferences. In the streams used as sources of water supply, the mean apparent ABS was less than 0.2 ppm on the average. These results confirmed the presence of ABS in receiving waters, which, given the findings of the earlier projects, must have surprised no one. More significantly, the levels of ABS reported were apparently no cause for alarm. But the industry was leaving nothing to chance, and it sponsored another project "concerned with developing effective and economic means for removing trace quantities of ABS from water supplies, should this ever become desirable."[38]

This project was carried out by Charles E. Renn, professor of sanitary engineering at Johns Hopkins University, and Mary F. Barada, his research assistant.[39] They studied the abilities of a number of materials to adsorb ABS, including garden soils, river silts, china clay, diatomite, silica gel, calcium carbonate, oil emulsions, powdered and granulated paraffin, and activated carbon. Activated carbon proved to be the best adsorber, its performance depending upon the variety of carbon used. With a carbon commonly employed in treatment plants, though not the best adsorber, about 40 mg/1 was required to remove 90 percent of an original ABS concentration of 0.2 mg/1, and 95 mg/1 to remove 90 percent of the ABS in a 2.0 mg/1 solution. The lower concentration represented peak ABS values for heavily polluted rivers, and the higher fell in the range of treated sewage effluent. Activated carbon was expensive and in terms of normal usage these carbon concentrations were high.[40]

With the continued financial support of the AASGP, Renn and Barada went on to study the effectiveness of conventional water treatment processes in removing ABS from raw water supplies. The industry's concern is seen in Renn and Barada's remark that "it is essential that any emergency regime for removing foaming concentrations of synthetic detergents from raw waters be compatible with other measures used in routine water treatment, especially with those available for handling the emergencies of low flow and gross pollution."[41]

Meanwhile, as noted, the levels of ABS reported in surface waters were no cause for alarm. It was quite another matter, however, when the presence of ABS in groundwater was reported. As one knowledgeable observer stated at the time, pollution of groundwater was much more serious than pollution of surface water. "Underground waters move more slowly; it may take months or even years before contamination appears; but once it has occurred, it may require as much or more time before the water is free again from contamination."[42]

Contamination of groundwater by synthetic detergents was first reported in 1958 in Suffolk County, Long Island, New York, an area where householders obtained their water from wells on their properties. An investigation of the situation in Suffolk County "was prompted by general complaints relative to taste, odor and frothing of water from the wells. The history relative to frothing led to analysis for syndets."[43] A report issued in midsummer, 1958, confirming the contamination of groundwater supplies by detergents from cesspools in heavily populated areas, was publicized in the *New York Times*. At a subsequent meeting held on August 14 to discuss the growing pollution threat to the county's groundwater table—which was replenished by precipitation and was the county's only source of potable water—John M. Flynn, a public health engineer in the county's department of health, exhibited two bottles of well water that contained enough detergent to form suds when shaken.[44] Flynn said that although the contamination caused the water to be distasteful he could not say whether or not it was a health hazard. But he added that detergents would not decompose in cesspools and would, in seeking the groundwater table, actually break down natural filter barriers in the soil, thereby allowing sewage to travel further than it otherwise would. George Moore of the New York State Health Department asserted that the problem was "serious," not only in Suffolk County but elsewhere in the state.

Flynn and two colleagues in the county department of health, Aldo Andreoli and August A. Guerrera, studied a residential area in the town of Babylon. In this area of approximately seventy-two acres, the average plot size was sixty by one hundred feet, and there were 5 to 6 homes per acre. The wells of 186 homes were tested for anionic detergent using the methylene blue method. In sixty (32 percent) of the wells, detergents were detected in varying amounts: twelve contained a concentration between 0.1 and 0.4 ppm, twenty-five between 0.4 and 0.9 ppm, seventeen between 0.9 and 1.4 ppm, and six greater than 1.4 ppm.[45] In some instances wells in which no detergents were detected in November, 1957, showed their presence in March, 1958. In no case was a reduction of detergent in a contaminated well observed during the same period.

Examination of the relationship of well depth to concentration of ABS indicated a decrease in concentration with increase in depth. Although increasing the depths of wells thus appeared to offer a solution to the problem, the investigators believed that the only gain would be time and that ABS would ultimately reappear, as had happened with other wells in the county that had been deepened.

Distance from cesspool was measured for 111 of the wells studied. Of 12 wells sixty-five feet or more from a cesspool, 2 showed "traces" of detergent; whereas, of 99 wells less than sixty-five feet from a cesspool, 46 showed such traces. Sixty-five feet was the study's cut-off point because it was the county department of health's recommended minimum distance between well and cesspool. Spot sampling of wells in an area of Suffolk County where wells and cesspools had been installed in conformance with county standards showed that 7 out of 17 wells contained detergents. A study of an area contaminated by detergents from a launderette in Brookhaven—also in Suffolk County—had shown traces of detergents as much as five hundred feet from their source.

To determine the concentration at which detergents created an unpleasant taste in water, Flynn and his coworkers followed two procedures.[46] First, twenty-six housewives from homes with contaminated wells were interviewed. The wells had detergent concentrations varying from 0.25 to 2.5 ppm. Results indicated that about 10 percent of the housewives whose wells had a detergent concentration of less than 1 ppm reported an off-taste, while all housewives whose wells had a concentration of 1.5 ppm or more reported such a taste. Second, using a standard household detergent, tap water (apparently assumed to be free of detergents) samples were made containing detergent concentrations varying from 1 to 3 ppm. A control sample containing no detergent was included in the group. Without knowing the concentrations of the samples, twenty-three members of the Suffolk County Department of Health tested them for taste. A majority of the testers began to detect an off-taste at 2.0 ppm, while 35 percent reported an off-taste at 1.0 ppm. Six individuals reported no off-taste—which was variously described by the others as oily, fishy, and, frequently, perfume-like—in any of the samples.

During the next five years the contamination of Suffolk County groundwater by detergents was a problem that received considerable national attention. In July, 1959, a joint committee of county supervisors and the Suffolk County Water Authority was formed to study the problem.[47] The committee's chair stated that although consultants on sanitation and geology agreed that there was no immediate health menace from detergents in drinking water— "the limits of human tolerance is many times higher than the 1 ppm concentration of syndets at which foaming occurs"—more exhaustive studies of their effects would have to be made. In December, 1961, the *New York Times* reported that "a glass of water drawn from a private well tap at a Town of

Babylon home recently overflowed with suds before the glass was half full of water."[48] An accompanying photograph of the glass of foam and water was captioned "Detergent Cocktail." Outside Long Island, other areas of New York state also began to experience the problem. In April, 1962, Gov. Nelson A. Rockefeller appointed a commission to "consider the effects of the continuously increasing discharge of detergents into the underground upon the health, safety and welfare of the present and future populations and the dangers that such discharges of waste may create to the adequacy and safety of the water supply."[49] Two weeks later *Time* magazine ran a photograph of a glass of sudsy water being drawn from a kitchen faucet and commented, "In many suburban areas, such as New York's Suffolk County, a glass of water from the tap is likely to have a detergent head on it like a schooner of beer." *Time* added that while most experts agreed that "syndet-spiked" drinking water so far posed no serious health threat, there were some who anticipated the worst if "syndets keep pouring into the ground." It quoted a "self-appointed Paul Revere of detergent danger," Edward J. Zimmer, director of Chicago's plumbing testing laboratory: "You know how detergents get in under the grease and soil and lift them right off your plate? Well, you get too much detergent in your system from drinking water and the same thing happens—it lifts the mucous lining right off your stomach and intestines and esophagus." However, *Time* noted that others were insisting that "the syndet menace, like the fallout danger [from atomic bomb tests, another contemporary concern], is vastly exaggerated."[50]

In 1960 a U.S. Public Health Service (USPHS) official noted groundwater pollution by synthetic detergents in twelve other states: Alabama, Connecticut, Florida, Kansas, Massachusetts, Minnesota, New Mexico, New Jersey, Pennsylvania, Rhode Island, Virginia, and Wisconsin.[51] ABS concentrations of at least 0.1 ppm had been found in 357 of the 976 well waters examined in these states and New York. Concentrations of 4 ppm or more were reported in at least three cases. Sources of pollution now included, in addition to cesspools, oxidation ponds for treatment of municipal sewage, streams receiving sewage, holding ponds for industrial and commercial wastes, and facilities for waste disposal from commercial laundries.

During 1959, Rhode Island's department of health found detergent in water samples from 72 wells throughout the state.[52] The detergent's presence was first indicated by the formation of foam when the samples were shaken and then confirmed by analysis. A Wisconsin study revealed that anionic-type detergents were present in 32 percent of 2,167 privately owned, shallow wells tested.[53] Moreover, the data showed that as the concentration of detergents increased in these waters, the percentage of bacteriologically unsafe waters became larger, until the group of waters with 3 to 10 mg/1 of detergents had nearly five times as many bacteriologically unsafe waters as the group free of detergents. Even when less than 1.0 mg/1 of detergent was present, the percentage of bacteriologically unsafe waters was more than doubled. In Minnesota, in the Minneapolis–Saint Paul area, 13,800 (22 percent) of 63,000 wells tested were found to contain measurable quantities of surfactants.[54] By 1963 the Assistant Surgeon General of the United States, Dr. Gordon E. McCallum, was reporting that ABS was "now showing up in the ground and surface water in every populated area in this country and in Europe."[55] He questioned whether widespread use of ABS should have been permitted when it had been introduced after World War II.

It was within this context[56] that the AASGP's Research Steering Committee began its second major phase of work. This would include doing literature searches, cooperating with some organizations investigating the problem of groundwater pollution by detergents, keeping in touch with others, and carrying out its own research projects. The industry would leave no stone unturned.

Given the presence of ABS in drinking water, the two most urgent questions concerned its removal and its toxicity to humans. The industry's Research Steering Committee began by searching the scientific literature for toxicity studies of detergents, a subject with which the industry had apparently hitherto not concerned itself. A considerable amount of information was found, although it was concerned primarily with acute toxicity, that is, with single dose or short-term feeding of detergents to experimental animals, as opposed to chronic toxicity studies based on long-term feeding. One study had involved humans.[57] Six men had been fed a purified alkyl aryl sulfonate at a rate of 100 mg/day, the equivalent of two liters of water containing 50 ppm ABS per day, for four months. The men experienced no change in weight, and only two reported an effect on their appetites. Throughout the four months, blood and urine analyses were normal. The Research Steering Committee argued that these and other results all indicated that men and animals could tolerate relatively high concentrations of ABS in drinking water or food without ill effect. It noted that even in feeding studies in which concentrations of ABS reached high enough levels to produce noticeable effects, the effects generally took the form of temporary gastrointestinal disturbances resulting rather from the irritant action common to all soaps and anionic detergents than from any true toxic action. The committee concluded that "although future surveillance of the whole situation is, of course, desirable, it seems definite at this time [June, 1960] that, based on a conservative assessment, ABS can be consumed at concentrations at least several times those presently found in drinking waters without producing any long-term, physiological effects."[58]

Meanwhile, individual member companies of the AASGP had been conducting chronic toxicity studies on animals. T. W. Tusing, O. E. Paynter, and

D. L. Opdyke of Hazleton Laboratories, Falls Church, Virginia, a contract research and development company specializing in biological and applied chemical research, and Miami Valley Laboratories, Procter and Gamble Company, Cincinnati, Ohio, undertook to extend the earlier investigations and determine whether the long-term ingestion of ABS in amounts exceeding those present in environmental sources would constitute a hazard.[59] In a feeding study, rats received 0.1 percent (1,000 ppm) and 0.5 percent (5,000 ppm) of ABS in their diet during a two-year period, which is almost the full lifespan of a rat. No adverse effects were found in analyses of growth, reproduction, survival, food consumption, hematologic values, blood chemistry, and urine. Furthermore, microscopic evaluation of tissues revealed no pathologic changes resulting from the consumption of ABS, and only scattered differences were observed in organ-to-body weight ratios. In a second two-year study rats were administered ABS in their drinking water at a level representing at least a five-hundred-fold exaggeration in daily consumption, on a body weight basis, over the possible figure for humans of less than 1 ppm. Once again no adverse effects were observed in regard to survival, growth, food consumption, organ weights, hematologic values, blood chemistry, or urine analyses; and a histopathologic survey of the essential organ systems revealed no evidences of toxicity. Increased organ-to-body weight ratios occurred in the livers of males and the empty ceca of females, but these differences were not accompanied by microscopic evidence of toxic changes. Thus lifetime administration of ABS to rats by two routes had produced no evidence of toxicity as judged by the criteria evaluated. The experimenters concluded that "to the extent that animal tests provide a basis for the assay of toxicity to humans, it would appear that these investigations assure that considerable amounts of ABS (much in excess of the amounts that might find their way into drinking water) could be consumed over long periods without harm."[60]

Although the results of these studies were quite clear-cut, the Research Steering Committee recommended a two-year feeding study in dogs. This recommendation was based on the opinion of toxicologists, including those in the Food and Drug Administration, that studies in two species, one of them not a rodent, were desirable in a complete toxicological investigation.[61] The study was carried out at an independent testing laboratory. During a two-year period beagles were fed 1,300 grams of food containing up to 1,000 ppm of ABS per week with no discernible effects on the health of any of the animals as determined by outward appearance or medical examination of the vital internal organs.[62] Those beagles which consumed the maximum amount of ABS, 130 grams, over a two-year period weighed approximately 10 kilograms each. This rate of consumption was equivalent to that of a man weighing 70 kilograms consuming 910 grams, or about 2 pounds, of ABS over a two-year period. For such a man ingesting 5 kilograms of water per day to take in 2 pounds of ABS, the concentration of ABS would have to be 250 ppm, a figure hundreds of times that found in practice.

The steering committee itself had, through a technical subcommittee formed in 1959, surveyed the concentration of ABS in municipal drinking water supplies. The supplies of thirty-two cities across the nation, having a combined population of about one-eighth of the national population, were examined. One-quart samples were taken in summer when rainfall and, therefore, runoff was low; in early winter when runoff was relatively low; and in spring when runoff was high. The samples came principally from rivers, but also from wells, two of the Great Lakes, reservoirs, and, in the case of Boulder, Colorado, a glacier. Analysis was made for ABS using the methylene blue method, which, as noted, is subject to positive interferences when used in analyzing surface water samples. Nevertheless, the ABS concentrations in the drinking waters tested were found to be "extremely low." [63] They ranged from zero to 0.14 ppm, with an average value of 0.024 ppm. Ninety-eight percent of the samples had a concentration below 0.10 ppm. As was not unexpected, the average concentration was highest during the summer (0.034 ppm) and lowest during the spring (0.015 ppm). If, as appeared from the above mentioned study on beagles, 250 ppm ABS would not be toxic to humans, then there seemed to be little immediate need for concern over the concentrations of ABS in the nation's drinking water.

By 1961, reports of drinking water supplies contaminated by detergents were becoming more common. In revising its drinking water standards that year, the USPHS for the first time set an upper limit of 0.5 ppm ABS in drinking water. [64] The limit was set for reasons of aesthetics as opposed to toxicity:

> . . . higher concentrations may cause the water to exhibit undesirable taste and foaming. Concentrations of ABS above 0.5 mg/l are also indicative of questionably [sic] undesirable levels of other sewage pollution.
>
> An ABS concentration of 0.5 mg/l in drinking water, in terms of a daily human intake of two liters, would give a safety factor of the order of 15,000, calculated on the results of subacute and two-year tests on rats fed diets containing ABS. [65]

In 1962 the USPHS published a study of the water supplied to 139 cities across the nation from 194 sources. The types of supply were: 147 surface, 39 ground, and 8 ground and surface. In 165 sources tested for ABS, its concentration was found to range from zero to 0.640 ppm, with a mean value of 0.054 ppm. [66] Only two sources exceeded the USPHS standard of 0.5 ppm.

The first published paper on the Suffolk county, New York, situation reported that water polluted by detergents had oily, fishy, or perfume-like tastes. But tests made in the same year by the USPHS at the Robert A. Taft Sanitary Engineering Center at Cincinnati, Ohio, the largest research enterprise of its kind in the world, showed that the odor of ABS was rarely detectable at concentrations of less than 1,000 ppm and that only very sensitive individuals could taste ABS in water at concentrations as low as 16 ppm.[67] About the same time members of the AASGP's Research Steering Committee also carried out tests in their own laboratories using panels of tasters.[68] The conclusions were quite similar in all laboratories: the threshold level for taste of ABS was in excess of 40 ppm and the threshold for odor was somewhat higher. All test panels reported that there was no fishy or oily taste and that the presence of ABS was indicated rather by a sensation in the mouth.

Although ABS itself at the concentrations that might be found in potable water did not appear to affect the odor or taste of the water, the possibility existed that ABS might intensify the odors or tastes of other impurities present in water. To check this possibility the Research Steering Committee sponsored work at an outside consulting laboratory known for its competence in classifying flavors.[69] The laboratory tested whether or not the addition of ABS at levels from 0.1 to 5.0 ppm would intensify (1) sulfidy, (2) fishy, and (3) chlorinated tastes. These tastes were created by, respectively, (1) hydrogen sulfide, (2) trimethylamine, cod liver oil, or a mixture of hydrogen sulfide and trimethylamine, and (3) chlorophenol or heavily chlorinated municipal water. In no case was the taste intensified. The laboratory also reported that while ABS at low concentrations did not contribute to the taste or odor of water, it caused an "astringent" or "fuzzy" sensation in the mouth at 5–10 ppm.

Studies conducted by Jesse M. Cohen of the USPHS at the Taft Sanitary Engineering Center in Cincinnati using solutions of purified ABS in distilled water showed that concentrations up to 1,000 mg/l had virtually no odor. However, much lower concentrations were detected by taste; 50 percent of a panel of tasters detected ABS at a concentration of 60 mg/l. The lowest detectable concentration, 16 mg/l, was detected by only 5 percent of the panel members. In finished water the ABS concentration rarely exceeded a few tenths of a milligram per liter. Cohen therefore concluded that in such water ABS alone could not be the cause of either taste or odor. "ABS is always accompanied by other contaminants from domestic or industrial sources, however, and the reported taste and odor must be attributed to these contaminants."[70] Thus, as with toxicity, so with taste and odor, ABS did not constitute a problem in the concentrations in which it was found in drinking water.

As noted above, in August, 1958, John M. Flynn had suggested that detergents would break down natural filter barriers in the soil, thereby facilitating the travel of sewage from cesspools to wells. If this were true then sewage bacteria, in addition to detergents, could be in drinking water. The industry was concerned, but the Research Steering Committee did not initiate its own investigation of this possibility, as a study of the problem had been undertaken by the USPHS at its Taft Sanitary Engineering Center.[71] The committee did, however, meet with the Taft Center's investigators to discuss the center's work. In addition, to help it in its own investigations of the groundwater problem and to maintain contact with local, state, and federal public health authorities, the committee retained J. C. Dietz, a former professor of sanitary engineering at the University of Illinois, as a consultant. Through early 1961 his work consisted largely of on-the-spot investigation of reported instances of groundwater contamination in order to learn more about the effects of soil type and geological factors on underground migration of contaminants of all kinds.

The Taft Center's report, published in January of 1962, described how over an eighteen-month period the influence of ABS on the movement of coliform organisms through water-saturated Ohio sands had been studied. The principal finding was that ABS in concentrations up to 10 ppm did not have a significant influence on the movement of coliform organisms through homogenous sands that were saturated with water.[72] These organisms traveled much more slowly than ABS, not penetrating much beyond six feet in 417 days when the water was moving at 0.4 feet per day. In spite of this apparent reassurance, a report on a symposium held by the Society for Industrial Microbiology at the end of 1962 stated that where detergents made their way into drinking water, "the possible simultaneous entry of intestinal viruses [was] considered a real public health hazard."[73]

The industry's response to the foaming problem created by detergents was to examine it thoroughly; they were interested in saving ABS, a highly successful, widely used, and relatively inexpensive surfactant. But their series of sponsored research projects, carried out under what I have called their first phase of research, showed that there seemed to be no way of preventing up to 40 percent of ABS from passing undegraded through sewage treatment plants into receiving waters. In certain instances that meant ABS would be present in sources used for drinking water, a problem that was compounded when ABS began to show up in groundwater supplying wells. A second, somewhat different, phase of research conducted by the industry's Research Steering Committee showed, however, that at the levels encountered in drinking water, almost universally below the upper limit of 0.5 ppm set by the USPHS, ABS constituted no threat to human health.

The industry's Research Steering Committee had expeditiously examined every facet of the detergent pollution problem, either by itself or by cooperating with other bodies conducting their own studies. The committee's connections with ORSANCO, the USPHS, and the AWWA have been noted. It also maintained liaison with the British Government's Standing Committee on Synthetic Detergents, whose activities are the subject of the next chapter.[74] On occasion it appeared that the committee's involvement with other bodies went beyond what would be considered proper. For example, the ORSANCO Detergent Subcommittee published a major report in 1963 stating that "at the levels presently encountered, ABS does not itself pose any public health problems, and *can be tolerated in ground water supplies,* but it would be constructive to eliminate it or remove it because of the frothing tendency" (emphasis added).[75] This subcommittee was chaired by Frank J. Coughlin, and included as members H. V. Moss and P. J. Weaver; all three had chaired the industry's Research Steering Committee.

It was only with reluctance that the industry admitted that detergents caused the foaming problem, and even then it stressed that detergents were only a small part of the burgeoning water pollution problem that had led to the National Conference on Water Pollution held in December, 1960. The industry endorsed the conference's recommendation that "the construction of municipal waste treatment facilities should be expanded immediately, with continued increases to keep up with population growth and to abate the backlog of pollution by 1970."[76] In the industry's view this was the proper solution to problems of groundwater pollution in such areas as Suffolk County, New York.[77] In the meantime the presence of ABS was held to have a positive aspect. Representatives of industry, including F. J. Coughlin, frequently claimed, "While ABS per se is not a desirable additive for water, some water pollution control people recognize the indisputable fact that ABS is an index of pollution of sewage origin and that the foaming tendencies of ABS are a warning of other potentially more serious pollution."[78]

Despite these defenses, responsible people were putting pressure on the industry. At the National Conference on Water Pollution in 1960, Rolf Eliassen, professor of sanitary engineering at MIT, commented:

> In order to leave no stones unturned, this conference must ask the chemical industry: "What are the chances of changing the character of the synthetic chemicals which contribute to water contamination?" The old-fashioned soaps were completely destroyed by microorganisms in waste treatment plants and streams so that no problems were encountered in water treatment plants. Synthetic detergents, as presently distributed to domestic consumers, are only partly degradable by microorganisms, due to the configurations of the detergent molecule. It should not be difficult for the chemical industry to develop a different series of compounds and produce some which could be broken down, and still be relatively inexpensive, as are the present soaps and detergents.[79]

In discussing Eliassen's paper, Richard Hazen, a consulting engineer, declared that Eliassen's third class of contaminants, which included detergents, other synthetic chemicals, and radioactive wastes, "is of course the one giving the most concern." He explained: "We are concerned not because the immediate concentration of these wastes is perilous, but because we do not know the long-range effects of these contaminants. We may not know some of these effects for generations."[80] By 1962 the industry was admitting that surfactants that could be more rapidly degraded by sewage bacteria would have beneficial effects, including reduction of foam on sewage treatment plant aeration tanks and receiving waters, as well as reduction of surfactant in groundwater.[81]

While there had been no public outcry about the detergent problem, it was becoming clear that something would have to be done about it soon. A symposium on synthetic detergents in water and sewage systems at the meeting in December of 1962 of the American Association for the Advancement of Science heard that numerous industries were "now being adversely affected by the frothing and foaming which result from the presence of finite and measurable amounts of surface active agents in water supplies."[82] A few months later William R. Samples, a civil engineer at the California Institute of Technology, was testing a potential solution to the foaming problem at Los Angeles's Hyperion Sewage Treatment Plant.[83] Samples began with the knowledge that while detergents used for washing purposes were generally of the anionic type, those used in mouthwashes, disinfectants, shampoos, and swimming pool cleaners were of the cationic type. He hypothesized that by injecting the latter type into wastewater loaded with the former type, negatively charged molecules would pair with positively charged ones to form neutral molecules which would not cause foaming. Adding alum would cause the resulting molecules to coagulate and sink to the bottom of a holding tank from which they would be removed mechanically.

Most of the activity associated with the detergent industry's first phase of research occurred at the in-house level. With the detection of detergents in groundwater, however, the detergent pollution problem had assumed a more troublesome aspect and become more of a public issue, a trend that would intensify.

IV

The British Experience with Synthetic Detergents

The extensive replacement of traditional soap by synthetic detergents also occurred in other countries, notably the United Kingdom and the Federal Republic of Germany, about the same time as in the United States. Like the United States, these countries experienced problems with foaming and became concerned about the possible effects on humans of ingesting detergents from drinking water. There are several reasons for examining Great Britain's experience. First, detergent technology was and would continue to be an international technology, in that what was successful in one country would soon be adopted in others. Second, some U.S. detergent companies had branches in Britain, and were therefore affected by and interested in what occurred there in regard to detergents. Indeed, the American Association of Soap and Glycerine producers would, through its members' related companies in Britain, be indirectly involved in the British study of the problem. Finally, consideration of the British activities is of interest because of the manner in which the problem was addressed there. In regard to the public types of opposition to controversial technologies, the British took a distinctive approach: the national government orchestrated the investigation of the problem from 1953. By 1960 the British had begun to alleviate the problem through the use of new surfactants.

Widespread foaming on rivers first attracted British public attention to the undesirable effects of synthetic detergents. A letter to the editor published in the *Times* early in 1953 noted that

> The reports in your columns recently of certain legal proceedings relating to the River Lea revealed the apparently undisputed fact that its waters are so heavily polluted with detergents or wetting agents that at times masses of foam several feet deep ride on its surface. This river is one of the important sources of the supply of water for domestic and other purposes in certain districts of London, and the question must insistently arise: What will be the effect upon

the health of the people who consume over a long period of time even limited quantities of detergents or surface active agents? So far as I am aware, the normal methods of purification are incapable or removing these chemicals from the water; and it may be that no practicable method of eliminating them has ever been devised.[1]

Some ten days later the water examination committee of the Metropolitan Water Board reported that while it had no "real" evidence for believing that the board's waters were in any immediate danger from the presence of synthetic detergents, it could not but view the future with anxiety.[2] In accepting the committee's report the board decided to approach the Ministry of Housing and Local Government "regarding the serious nature of the problem and suggesting the desirability of researches being initiated." In noting that the board's action "reflected a growing public opinion," the *Times* suggested that the "approach most likely to be effective, and therefore to command public confidence, would be a triple alliance of manufacturers, water authorities, and [physicians] to tackle the problem, if there is one, and to reassure the public if there is not."[3]

On May 12, 1953, Harold Macmillan, Minister of Housing and Local Government, appointed a Committee on Synthetic Detergents, composed of governmental, industrial, and academic representatives, "to examine and report on the effects of the increasing use of synthetic detergents and to make any recommendations that seem desirable with particular reference to the functioning of the public health services."[4] The committee issued an interim report in February, 1954, followed by a full report in December, 1955. At the outset of its work the committee established that the use of synthetic detergents was causing several different concerns.[5] Fears had been expressed that detergents might give rise to dermatitis and other dangers to health, and there had also been concern about their possible effects on household appliances and plumbing. None of these was ever a serious consideration in the United States. However, as in the United States, detergents were held responsible for excessive foaming and possibly reduced operational efficiency at sewage treatment plants. Finally, in consequence of the latter concern, there was the further concern about the purity of rivers, particularly of some used as sources of public water supply, and into which the effluents from sewage works were discharged. The committee resolved to assess the nature, magnitude, and implications of these problems and to recommend how they should be dealt with by the permanent bodies specially concerned.

Those Britons chiefly subjected to the hazard of dermatitis caused by synthetic detergents were housewives and the employees of laundries and catering establishments. The committee found, however, that the incidence of skin trouble attributable to detergents was no higher than that previously due to the use of soap products, alkalis, and allied preparations. In regard to acute toxicity, the committee noted that most of the synthetic detergents used in Britain were based on anionic surfactants. It had found no evidence to show that these or the builders usually incorporated with them would, if swallowed by mistake, have serious effects. Moreover, most household detergents were sold as powders, meaning accidental swallowing of any sizeable quantity would presumably be difficult. The committee therefore did not anticipate that any material risk of acute toxicity by ingestion would arise from continued extensive use of detergents.[6] The committee also considered the possible effects on humans of the ingestion of repeated small doses of detergents (or of some of their ingredients) over a prolonged period. Such doses might come either from imperfectly rinsed crockery or cutlery washed in detergent solutions, or by consumption of water derived from rivers into which sewage effluents containing detergent residues had been discharged. The committee concluded, however, that no evidence existed that would justify its regarding detergents based on anionic or nonionic surfactants as harmful in this respect. Nevertheless, it cautioned that as observations would have to be made over long periods of time, and as it was not possible to argue with certainty from animal experiments to man, the possibility of harm would need to be kept under review.

With regard to household plumbing, the committee pointed to the fact that where detergents were brought into contact with metals, their excellent cleaning properties might, by removing films of grease or soap curd, either present the possibility of corrosion or expose corrosion previously hidden.[7] It suggested that the growing use of detergents might well increase the importance of avoiding, in plumbing, both the use of easily corrodible metals and the use together of electrochemically dissimilar metals. The committee was aware of instances in Britain and the United States of foam backing up waste pipes through traps, and into dwellings on the lower floors of high blocks of apartments. However, this problem did not appear to be either extensive or severe.

Concerning foam in sewage treatment plants, it was quite another story. The committee noted that from 1949 new household synthetic detergents based on alkyl aryl sulfonates had been introduced. Almost immediately, aeration tanks at sewage treatment plants using the activated sludge process for secondary treatment became covered with a white persistent foam, sometimes several feet deep. A propensity to cause copious and persistent foam in the washtub was a leading characteristic of the new detergents. The coincidence in time between their introduction and the onset of foam at sewage plants seemed to the committee to leave little room for doubt that one was the cause of the other.[8] Thus, in contrast to the United States, where for several more years industry spokesmen would continue to deny a connection between the presence of synthetic detergents and foam in sewage treatment plants, in Britain the connection was acknowledged from 1956 by all parties concerned, including the industry.

The committee considered foam at sewage treatment plants to be mainly a nuisance, but also a source of danger. In excessive amounts, foam could prevent maintenance staff from walking along footways between tanks in carrying out their necessary duties; and upon collapsing, foam left behind a residue that was slippery underfoot. Where foam spilled over onto surrounding land, it left a similar unpleasant residue that killed grass and plants, and made the sewage works unsightly, dirty, and malodorous. When blown away from the plant it could be a nuisance where it landed, and as it contained sewage matter it could be a danger to public health. "It certainly gives rise to complaint, and in our opinion rightly so," warned the committee. "We consider that its continued production at sewage works should not be tolerated indefinitely." Regarding a solution, the committee suggested that if the surfactants incorporated in detergents could be made to respond more readily to biological oxidation during sewage treatment, many of the causes for anxiety about the effects of their presence in sewage would disappear.[9]

Although foam in sewage works was the most obvious and perhaps the most immediate problem caused by the presence of synthetic detergents in sewage, to the committee it was not necessarily the most serious. Questions remained about the extent to which detergent residues persisted through sewage treatment and of the effects they might have, first on the treatment processes themselves and then in receiving rivers and waterworks downstream. The committee was aware that the breakdown or removal of any substance during the second, main (or biological) stage of sewage treatment depended on the existence and growth of bacteria that could use it as food, and upon the production, during the process, of surfaces upon which the substance could be adsorbed. It also knew that most, if not all, natural organic substances could be destroyed by bacteria, and that bacteria would also attack some organic compounds that so far as was known were not produced in nature. Frequently a biological filter, or an activated sludge, had no significant action on these substances at first, but ultimately a suitable bacterial flora developed, after which oxidation took place quickly and reliably. Such a system was said to have become acclimatized. The committee found it significant that synthetic detergents of the type in use had been present in sewage in Britain for several years, and yet reports from all parts of the country had shown surfactants that must have derived from them were still being discharged with sewage effluents. It therefore seemed that sewage treatment systems had not become acclimatized to surfactants even after several years. This appeared also to be the case in other countries. In Britain the concentration of surfactant remaining in sewage effluent after biological oxidation was often as much as half or more of that in crude sewage. The average concentrations in effluents from ten sewage works tested ranged from 1 to 12 ppm, six of them lying between 3 and 6 ppm. The committee considered all of these to be appreciable amounts.[10]

In regard to the sewage treatment process, the committee found that alkyl aryl sulfonate appeared to reduce the efficiency of biological oxidation plants. Although the circumstance required further investigation, they surmised that any adverse effect would probably be reduced or eliminated if the surfactant could be broken down during the purification process.[11]

Though the committee had found little direct evidence linking detergents to foaming on rivers, it did note that such foaming was mostly attributed by the river boards to the presence in the water of detergents or their residues. Certain spectacular instances of foaming had clearly coincided with increased sales of detergents in the districts concerned.[12] The committee also noted that few attempts had been made to control foaming on rivers by measures taken on rivers themselves. It added that the use of defoamants would be open to the serious objection that it would involve, in effect, polluting the river water; and in any event the mere suppression of foam on a river, without removing the original cause of its occurrence, might in the long run be a mistake.

It seemed clear from work already done that there would be certain rivers in which the presence of surfactants derived from synthetic detergents would reduce re-aeration. This would thus cause, other things being equal, a lowering of the concentration of dissolved oxygen in the water, which in the committee's view would be a tendency in the wrong direction. The committee suspected that the presence of surfactants in rivers, if it had a detectable effect on fish, was less likely to show itself by causing extensive mortality from time to time than by acting in conjunction with other adverse factors and so extending those parts of a polluted river in which fish could not live continuously. However, as with the possible effects of anionic surfactants on water vegetation, little was known or had been reported.[13]

In regard to water purification, the committee noted that besides being able to cause foam, synthetic detergents were excellent wetting, emulsifying, dispersing, and deflocculating agents. They had the ability at certain concentrations to maintain substances in a state of suspension in water, and in general were chemically stable, retaining these properties even in high dilution and over a wide range of pH. As the purification of water involved the removal by various means, including flocculation and precipitation, of as much material as possible, the effects of detergency clearly conflicted with the aims of water treatment. The committee recognized that where a public water supply was derived from rivers into which sewage effluents were discharged upstream, the drinking water drawn by consumers from the tap must already have begun to contain slight traces of surfactants. So the question arose as to whether or not these traces were harmful to consumers. The committee took

the view that evidence of ill effects would already have become available had
any short-term risk existed—since many millions of Britons must have been
drinking such water for some years—but it knew of no such evidence. However, the possible effects of repeated ingestion of even minute amounts over
a prolonged period was a different matter; the committee could not argue
merely from a lack of evidence over the last few years. [14] It was clearly desirable that the circumstance of having in "drinking water, a new added ingre-
dient of no apparent benefit and of unknown long-term effect," be kept under
review. [15]

The committee concluded that synthetic detergents offered both material
advantage and desirable convenience. However, these features went hand in
hand with the difficulties, expenses, and risks that the disposal of used detergents introduced. The advantages to consumers were immediate and obvious,
but they were "advantages of, in the last analysis, convenience and not necessity." [16] The disadvantages were indirect, variable, and imprecise; they
might not always immediately affect more than a limited section of the population, but they arose in public services vital to the health and welfare of the
community as a whole. It was for consideration, the committee stated,
whether the community could really afford, consistent with its safety, to pay
for the advantages in this way. If there were any possibility that the advantages the consumers wanted could be obtained at a lower cost in terms of risk
to the environmental services which protected the public, it should be pursued
as a matter of public importance.

In regard to the possibility of achieving biological oxidation of the alkyl
aryl sulfonates, the committee thought it conceivable that research might lead
to the development of desired bacterial flora by some deliberate means. While
the prospects of success could not be rated highly, the committee nevertheless
recommended that this possibility be investigated if resources were available.
At the same time, "an urgent investigation" should be made by manufacturers
into the feasibility of replacing existing surfactants by products of similar
efficiency but less resistance to known methods of sewage treatment. [17]

Having thoroughly reviewed the real and imagined problems associated
with the use of detergents, the committee recommended creating a permanent
advisory body on detergents. The Standing Technical Committee on Synthetic Detergents, composed of governmental and industrial representatives,
was subsequently appointed on January 9, 1957, by the Minister of Housing
and Local Government, Duncan Sandys, "to keep under review the difficulties, or risks of difficulty, arising in sewage works, rivers and water supply as
a result of the use of synthetic detergents; to encourage, and assist the coor-
dination of, appropriate research by manufacturers of detergents and intermediate materials, and by suitable public bodies, into methods by which
those difficulties, or risks of difficulty, could without an undue burden on

public funds be avoided or overcome; and to report progress at least once a year." [18]

Pressed by the recommendations of the first committee and by the creation of the standing committee, the detergent manufacturers sought a modified alkyl benzene sulphonate or some other surfactant more easily and completely broken down in sewage works practice. It was not an easy task. The difficulty was to formulate a detergent that could be made from a surfactant available in the requisite quantity and at a cost, if not as low as that of detergents in use, at least of the same order. It was also economically desirable to continue to use the bulk of the existing manufacturing plant, upon which large capital sums had been expended. Furthermore, the final retail product would have to be as acceptable to the housewife as those already on the market.

By this time it was known that products with highly branched side chains, such as those derived from propylene tetramer, were most resistant to bacterial attack, whereas products with straight side chains were largely destroyed during the course of an efficient bacteriological treatment. A search was begun by the Royal Dutch Shell Group for suitable petroleum fractions that could be used as side chains in the manufacture of alkyl benzene and that could be obtained in the very substantial quantities required and at reasonable cost. The thermal cracking of petroleum wax was found to yield a mixture of olefins which, on distillation, gave a fraction with properties and chain length required for the manufacture of alkyl benzenes. However, these olefins did not consist simply of straight-chain molecules, and they gave rise to alkyl benzenes with varying degrees of branching in the side chains, which usually also contained ring structures. Tests indicated a definite trend in the direction of greater residual 'hardness' as the number of methyl groups per molecule increased. (An alkylate with a completely straight side chain has two methyl groups per molecule, whereas an alkylate derived from propylene tetramer has some four or five methyl groups per molecule.) The trend toward hardness was more marked for dimethyl groups. [19] Study of the non-benzenoid ring content of the alkylate showed that the greater the number of non-benzenoid rings, the greater the degree of residual hardness. The Shell investigators therefore concluded that biodegradation was affected by the number of dimethyl groups per molecule and to a lesser extent by the total number of methyl groups and the ring content of the side chain.

By early 1958 a new surfactant, a straight-chain alkyl benzene sulfonate called Dobane JN sulfonate, had been developed by Shell. [20] It was prepared using the wax cracking process, and samples of it were made available to the British Standing Committee on Synthetic Detergents for testing. [21] (Down through 1963 the only large scale cracking of wax for detergent purposes would be carried out by the Royal Dutch Shell Group, which cracked several hundred thousand tons per year. [22]) Laboratory tests by the Metropolitan Water

Board and the Department of the Government Chemist substantiated work carried out by the manufacturers indicating that, compared to the alkyl benzene sulfonate in use (Dobane PT sulfonate or tetrapropylene benzene sulfonate), a much larger proportion of the new material was decomposed biologically. At the request of the standing committee, the Department of Scientific and Industrial Research agreed that its Water Pollution Research Laboratory should make comprehensive pilot-scale tests of the behavior of both the old and the new surfactants during sewage treatment. Once again results showed that a substantially greater proportion of the new material was removed. Under comparable conditions, with both activated sludge and biological filters, 94 percent of the new surfactant was destroyed as compared with 68 percent of the old. Furthermore, preliminary measurements of foaming indicated that the amount of foam produced by effluent from the treatment of sewage containing the new material was little more than that from effluents free of detergents.[23]

The manufacturers soon suggested to the standing committee that the value of the new material might be assessed with greater confidence if a full-scale trial were carried out in a suitable area.[24] It was quickly realized that for this to be done very considerable marketing problems would have to be overcome; nevertheless, the major companies, which together sold over 95 percent of the packaged detergent in Britain, agreed to participate in such a trial. Concerned that public knowledge of the trial might lead to some alteration in purchasing habits, which would affect the outcome of the experiment, the standing committee decided that during its initial stages the trial should be conducted without any public announcement.

The upper valley of the River Lea, in which the towns of Luton and Harpenden were situated, appeared to offer several advantages in conducting a full-scale trial. When approached, officials of the two local authorities readily agreed to cooperate in the trial. The River Lea rose near Luton and was still quite small when it received the town's sewage effluent. Three miles downstream from Luton it also received Harpenden's sewage effluent, and after flowing five more miles the river passed over a weir at Lemsford Mill where foam was always produced, occasionally in large amounts. The Lea was subsequently enlarged by several tributaries, after which a substantial part of its content was abstracted by London's Metropolitan Water Board.

The manufacturers agreed to start supplying detergents based on Dobane JN sulfonate to stores in the Luton area on August 1, 1958. Sewage and effluent sampling commenced at the beginning of June to provide two months' data before the changeover was initiated. Samples of settled sewage and final effluent were taken at both the Luton and the Harpenden sewage works. Coincidentally, from February, 1958, the Water Pollution Research Laboratory had been taking photographs of the Lea at Lemsford Mill and

Wheathampsted between 9:30 and 10:00 on Tuesday and Friday mornings. At the same time the laboratory took single samples of river water at these locations to determine its anionic surfactant content.[25]

Due to various problems, the Luton experiment, as the trial came to be known, had to be continued for more than two years, until July, 1960.[26] One unexpected difficulty had been securing the replacement of a sufficiently large proportion of the old surfactant by the new in the area draining to the Luton sewage works. The manufacturers were required to extend considerably their initial distribution area. However, by August, 1960, Dobane JN sulfonate constituted from 95 to 99 percent of the surfactant in various packaged detergent products on sale in the Luton area. One complication that was not overcome was that it had not been practicable to substitute Dobane JN sulfonate for the surfactant used in scouring powders. As the latter accounted for some 4 percent of the consumption of all synthetic detergents on a national scale, they had to be regarded as a significant source of hard detergent in Luton.

Results of the trial indicated that between June–July, 1958, and April–June, 1960, the concentration of surfactant in Luton's sewage effluent fell from about 3 to 2 ppm, that is, by one-third. During the latter period, sewage plant personnel determined that Dobane JN sulfonate constituted on the average about 73 percent of all surfactant in the Luton plant's settled sewage. Assuming that the removal of the old, hard surfactant at the plant was still about 66 percent, as determined from the data collected in 1958 just prior to the introduction of Dobane JN sulfonate, the standing committee calculated that some 85 percent of the Dobane JN sulfonate was removed in sewage treatment. Using this figure, they further deduced that complete substitution of the former surfactant by Dobane JN sulfonate would reduce the concentration of surfactant in Luton effluent to rather less than half the value observed before the introduction of Dobane JN, that is, from 3 to about 1.3 ppm. Overall, the standing committee concluded that Dobane JN sulfonate did not afford a complete solution to the problems arising from the use of synthetic detergents and that further improvement of detergents currently in use, including the development of new surfactants, was necessary.[27] Such was the apparent concern for secrecy on the part of the manufacturers that not only was nothing said in the annual reports of the standing committee that described the Luton experiment—about either the chemical nature of Dobane JN sulfonate or its manufacture—but its commercial name was not even used. It was referred to, variously, as the new, or soft, material.

Only in its 1962 annual report did the standing committee for the first time speak of "Dobane JN sulfonate."[28] It reiterated its view that it could not regard the softer detergents based on Dobane JN as a complete or satisfactory long-term solution, particularly in view of the marked upward trend in the use of synthetic detergents. The committee had learned that the manufacturing capacity for the new surfactant was sufficient to meet from 60 to 70 percent of the United Kingdom's requirements, but that any extension of this capacity would involve substantial capital outlay. Furthermore, an extension might be accompanied by the unavoidable production of associated materials in excess of the market requirements and thereby lead to an increase in the price of the basic detergent. The committee considered whether it should recommend to the Minister of Housing and Local Government that "suitable steps" be taken to ensure that only Dobane JN sulfonate, or some other surfactant at least as soft, should be sold in the United Kingdom. It reasoned, however, that any action taken should depend upon whether or not there were reliable prospects of more highly degradable surfactants becoming commercially available in the near future. The committee was satisfied that intensive research was being conducted by the industry to develop such surfactants, and it understood that there were indeed good prospects of one or more satisfactory surfactants being produced within the next two to three years. One company had recently decided to install a plant, to be in production before the end of 1963, to manufacture sulfated fatty alcohols from tallow. These were understood to be completely biodegradable and already being used, in admixture with alkyl benzene sulfonate, in a detergent formulation in the United States.[29] In the meantime the committee recommended that the existing plant be used to its full capacity.

The committee's anticipations were confirmed when Royal Dutch Shell announced in 1962 that it was constructing a plant for producing a straight side chain hydrocarbon that could be used to make an alkylate, Dobane JNO 36, from which a surfactant claimed to be 99 percent degradable could be manufactured. Shell researchers had sought a means of reducing or eliminating the dimethyl groups and the non-benzenoid ring structures from the side chain of the alkyl benzene.[30] By submitting the petroleum-base material before cracking to an extraction process with urea, they found it possible to produce olefins suitable for alkylation in which the non-benzenoid ring structures had been considerably reduced and the dimethyl groups virtually eliminated.

At the same time the industry was increasingly using another alkylate, Dobane JNX, softer than Dobane JN, as a surfactant base.[31] The industry informed the standing committee that on the basis of small-scale tests it was confident that the newer surfactants (Dobane JNX sulfonate, Dobane JNO 36 sulfonate, and fatty alcohol sulfate) would enable most, if not all, of the problems arising from the use of synthetic detergents falling under the committee's terms of reference to be solved. The committee nevertheless decided to have the new materials tested independently. Samples of both the surfactants themselves and the detergents manufactured from them were tested using small-scale techniques in the laboratories of the Government Chemist and the London Metropolitan Water Board. At the same time, the Water Pollution Research Laboratory conducted pilot-scale tests on the removal of the surfactants by the normal methods of sewage treatment. Of the three detergents tested, one was 20 percent Dobane JNX sulfonate, one 20 percent Dobane JNO 36 sulfonate, and the third 10 percent Dobane JNO 36 sulfonate and 10 percent fatty alcohol sulfate.

The tests carried out by the Government Chemist and the Metropolitan Water Board confirmed that Dobane JNO 36 sulfonate was biodegraded more rapidly and to a greater extent than the Dobane JNX sulfonate currently in use. It represented a further improvement on the original hard material, Dobane PT sulfonate, which still accounted for some 30 percent of the alkyl benzene sulfonate used.[32] The tests also showed the tallow alcohol sulphate to be quickly and completely biodegraded.

In previous pilot-scale tests at the Water Pollution Research Laboratory, the results obtained for the removal of Dobane PT and Dobane JN sulfonates were found to be in good agreement with the results subsequently obtained in actual practice at the Luton sewage works.[33] On the basis of this agreement the committee reasonably assumed that the results now obtained on the pilot-scale filters with the three new detergent formulations would indicate what could be expected at the Luton sewage works if the new detergents were sold in Luton. When detergents based only on Dobane PT sulfonate had been used in Luton, the effluent contained up to 4 ppm of surfactant, and the committee had calculated that the complete replacement of Dobane PT by Dobane JN sulfonate, which had not been possible, would have reduced the concentration of surfactant in the effluent to about 2 ppm.[34] The recent tests indicated that the exclusive use of Dobane JNO 36 sulfonate would further reduce the concentration of surfactant to half that obtained with Dobane JN sulfonate and would result in the Luton effluent having a detergent content of about 1 ppm. As the tallow alcohol sulfate surfactant seemed to be fully removed during sewage treatment, it appeared that if half the Dobane JNO 36 sulfonate were replaced by sulfate, the detergent residue in the Luton effluent would fall to about ½ ppm.

The Water Research Laboratory also tested the relative foaming tendencies of the effluents from the experimental plants using a standardized aeration technique and measuring the depth of foam formed. The results indicated that complete substitution of the new surfactants for the original hard surfactant would unquestionably reduce to a varying extent both the incidence and the degree of foaming in water courses.[35] The use of tallow alcohol sulfate alone seemed to offer a complete solution of the problem of foaming in rivers. However, the industry had informed the committee that when used alone this surfactant did not yield a satisfactory detergent powder (it would seem because of caking), although when mixed in equal proportions with an alkyl benzene sulfonate, such as Dobane JNO 36 sulfonate, it could yield such a powder. The committee stated that if such a mixture were shown to be commercially and economically feasible, it would certainly recommend that materials having an overall biodegradability not significantly less than this mixture should be used instead of the currently used alkyl benzene sulfonates. However, the committee could not say whether the full use of detergents of this level of biodegradability would or would not provide an acceptable final solution to the synthetic detergent pollution problem in Britain.

Thus by 1963 the British were making progress towards solving the detergent pollution problem. In Britain the in-house and public concerns about detergent pollution were intimately meshed, because the British government had acted quickly to address the problem as soon as it had arisen. The government's committees on detergents sought and received the close cooperation of the industry in the analysis of the problem as well as in seeking its solution. The combined efforts of government and industry led to the creation, large-scale testing, and commercial introduction of a second generation of petroleum-based detergents more highly degradable than the first. All of these activities were closely followed by the detergent industry in the United States, which was about to be brought to task at state and national government levels in connection with the detergent pollution problem.

V

U.S. Government Response
to the Detergent Pollution Problem

Britain was not the only European nation to suffer pollution by synthetic detergents. In 1959 the West German Bundestag created a committee to investigate detergent pollution. Acting on the committee's recommendation, the Bundestag in 1961 passed a law regulating detergents. A regulation issued under the law in 1962 required the industry to market from October, 1964, only detergents that were more than 80 percent degradable. The Bundestag's approach to solving the problem was favored by several Democrats in the United States Congress who introduced bills early in 1963 banning the manufacture of hard detergents within the United States after mid-1965. The U.S. detergent industry vigorously opposed the bills, insisting that it should be allowed to solve the detergent pollution problem voluntarily. Convinced that it could, the Congress acceded to the industry's wishes.

The post-war period in West Germany, as in Britain and the United States, had seen the widespread substitution of soap by synthetic detergents, such that by the early 1960s some 90 percent of all cleaning and washing agents were synthetic detergents.[1] These detergents were primarily of the anionic type, consisting of up to 80 percent of tetrapropylbenzosulfonate, referred to as TPBS in West Germany and less specifically as ABS in the United States. The two principal manufacturers of ABS in Germany, A. Huls and Rhein-preussen, employed methods developed in the United States.[2] Like Americans and Britons, Germans came to recognize that although ABS had excellent washing properties, it was biologically hard, being only about 25 percent degradable under West German sewage treatment processes, and thus generating various problems.[3]

The presence of ABS in sewage was found to reduce the efficiency of mechanically equipped purification plants and septic tanks. Furthermore, its presence in sewage plant effluents gave rise to considerable foam formation, especially following strong oxygenation in overfalls, turbines, and sluices.

Foam four meters deep had formed in some sluice chambers, and dangerous situations had arisen on rivers due to foam covering up navigational signals or making it impossible to see, and therefore rescue, anyone in danger of drowning. In addition, ABS was understood to be harmful to fish and other aquatic organisms, with the "damage and/or death limit" presumed to be about 10–15 mg/l. Many German communities obtained their drinking water from surface water, and during 1959, a year of low rainfall, such drinking water was found to contain up to 0.9 mg/l of detergent. As the West German Federal Ministry of Health later commented:

> Such drinking water may have an unaesthetic effect due to the foam formation, acquire a soapy taste, and thus its utilization may be restricted. Even though, according to the series of tests made to date [May 1963], harm to living persons has not yet been proved, it cannot be established with certainty at this point whether an intake of these substances over a prolonged period of time would be completely harmless. In any case, the steady introduction in this manner of foreign matter into the human body must be considered highly undesirable.[4]

Given these circumstances, a federal investigation was begun in West Germany in 1958. Subsequently, the Committee on Detergents and Water, composed of experts in hydrology and chemistry and representatives of the federal, land, and municipal governments, was created and charged with investigating the overall problems and numerous specific related questions. After intensive study, particularly of activated carbon adsorption, chemical precipitation, biological degradation, and foam removal, the committee recommended that for social and economic reasons the most effective procedure would be to prohibit the sale of hard detergents in a series of steps. Some deputies of the Bundestag subsequently drafted a bill on detergents that was enacted on September 5, 1961. The law's purpose was to achieve maximum decomposability of surfactants used in laundry and cleaning compounds.[5] It authorized the federal government "to establish, by a statutory ordinance requiring the consent of the Bundesrat, the requirements of decomposability with regard to detergents in washing and cleansing media, as well as the necessary methods of testing."[6] Such requirements had to be in keeping with the level of scientific and technical knowledge attained in the fields of detergent manufacture and sewage plant operation.

The first regulation under the law was issued on December 1, 1962, and stipulated that as of October 1, 1964, anionic surfactants in laundry and cleaning compounds sold on the market must be at least 80 percent biodegradable. A laboratory-scale waste treatment facility was created for determining the degree of biodegradability of detergents.[7] Not surprisingly, some detergent manufacturers had opposed the law. "However, upon investigation by the Committee on Detergents and Water and according to opinions expressed by prominent experts, their arguments were found to be contrary to fact."

Even before the law was enacted, the West German detergent industry had begun work on the production of softer detergents. By early 1963 H. J. Zimmer Verfahrenstechnik, a chemical research and development firm located in Frankfurt, had announced a new group of nonionic surfactants that it claimed was 100 percent biodegradable.[8] The four members of the group were the sugar esters of ricinoleic and mono-, di-, and trihydroxystearic acids, all hydroxy fatty acids. The new surfactants were low-foaming and non-toxic, and were based on relatively cheap and readily available materials—sugar and natural oils. Their detergent ability compared favorably with that of ABS. Zimmer, which was not a chemical producer, hoped to license the process for making the new surfactants and was said to be negotiating with several detergent companies, including one in the United States.

The American federal government, unlike its British and West German counterparts, created no special committee to study the pollution problems associated with ABS. That is not to say that the problems were ignored. To the contrary, as was apparent from the discussion in chapter 3 of the pollution of groundwater by synthetic detergents, the USPHS, through its Robert A. Taft Sanitary Engineering Center in Cincinnati, Ohio, closely monitored the situation. That discussion also showed that the detergent industry deliberately established contact with all organizations, including the USPHS, studying pollution by detergents. Given the Taft Center's activity and its familiarity with the industry's studies and concern, as will be seen further, the Department of Health, Education, and Welfare (HEW) saw no need to create a special committee to study pollution by detergents.

No member of Congress seems to have shown any interest in pollution by detergents until 1962, when Rep. Henry Reuss (Democrat, Wisconsin) requested the Library of Congress Legislative Reference Service to prepare a report on detergents and the problems they were causing. Reuss had been disturbed for some time "by the increasing pollution of both our surface and our underground waters by synthetic detergents." Wisconsin's governor, Gaylord Nelson, had recently directed the state's board of health to test water supplies for the presence of detergents. Detergents had subsequently been found in the underground supplies of sixty-four of the state's seventy-two counties.[9] The report requested by Reuss, entitled "Detergents—A Source of Pollution and What Is Being Done" and prepared by Edward Wise, senior specialist in science and technology, was issued on November 1, 1962.[10]

In addition to reporting briefly the British experience and Luton test results, Wise noted the parallel situation in West Germany and commented that its "method of solving the problems is interesting and bears close watching."[11] Within weeks Reuss was in Germany to talk with government officials and observe firsthand the pollution of such rivers as the Rhine and Neckar. He learned that the German equivalent of the U.S. HEW had worked with the detergent industry to develop more highly degradable detergents that would not pollute. However, these "efforts at a purely voluntary solution proved unsuccessful" and so the German law had been enacted.[12]

Wise issued a supplement, on December 11, 1962, to his earlier report. In it, he described the research efforts of both the U.S. government, primarily at the Taft Sanitary Engineering Center in Cincinnati, and the American detergent industry. He characterized the Soap and Detergent Association as "a driving force behind most of the research effort to better understand the problem and get at the facts." However, he concluded that "there is little doubt but that the total research program might be speeded up through such means as (1) added dollar support; (2) higher priority of emphasis; or (3) expression of governmental concern and interest in current programs and status."[13]

On January 17, 1963, Reuss, adopting the approach used in West Germany, introduced H.R. 2105. He explained that it was designed "to bar from interstate commerce, after June 30, 1965, all surface-active detergents [*sic*] which do not meet standards of decomposability to be set by the Surgeon General of the United States."[14] He anticipated that the Surgeon General would establish standards that initially would be similar to the German ones. In explaining why he had introduced his bill, Reuss made extensive use of the information in Wise's reports. He recounted how Long Island residents had found white suds in their tap water. "The thickness was such that before a container was half full of water, the suds already would have foamed out over the edge." Similar occurrences had been reported from around the nation, including heavily developed residential areas in Maryland and Virginia. To Reuss the cause of this "startling occurrence" in these different locations was the same. Laundry effluents or dishwater saturated with detergents had seeped through the ground and contaminated the sources of drinking water.[15] Reuss believed that once water became saturated with synthetic detergents, it stayed that way. Nature, he declared in the House of Representatives, is powerless to purify such water because ABS, "brought out of petroleum, is an artificial insert into the water cycle." Reuss noted that so far there was no evidence that detergents in the concentrations then found in water supplies were directly harmful to humans. However, these tentative conclusions were based on only two years of study, an inadequate time he thought in view of the "cumulative nature" of the synthetic detergent problem: "Syndets do not dissolve [degrade] in water and they are not subject to normal bacterial action. Detergents are now being added to our water supplies at an annual rate of increase of 5 per cent. At this rate, the present, apparently nontoxic level of detergents in our water supplies will be doubled in 14 years. It would be folly to ignore future dangers."[16] Reuss added that a publication in June of 1962 from the West German Institute for Water, Soil, and Air Hygiene had found "indications of cancer-producing effects of detergents in the water supply." Apart from a few other references to this finding, nothing further was heard about detergents, in any amounts, causing cancer.[17] Later Reuss would advance a more substantial argument against detergents, namely, the additional costs they incurred for municipalities in operating sewage treatment plants.[18] In his home city of Milwaukee, Wisconsin, the annual cost had been estimated at $50,000. Cleveland, Ohio, had reported an expenditure of $250,000 on spraying equipment that would reduce, though not eliminate, the foaming in its plant.

Reuss argued that industry had the capability of producing synthetic detergents so constituted that they would undergo the normal breakdown of waste products by either nature's bacterial processes or man's imitation, in sewage treatment plants, of those processes. He claimed that such detergents, presumably the sugar esters previously mentioned, had been successfully developed in West Germany, and said that H.R. 2105 was essentially aimed at helping, although "forcing" would have been a more appropriate word, the detergent industry in the United States to make the transition to "decomposable" detergents.[19]

Reuss was aware that ending the pollution of water by detergents would solve only one part of the overall water pollution problem. Yet, he reasoned, "detergent pollution presents a significant challenge because it presents us with the opportunity to deal with a specific source of pollution by specific measures that are wholly within our grasp. Therefore, we should not hesitate. We should take this step not for itself alone but also as a harbinger of other actions to assure our vital supply of pure water."[20] Many apparently agreed with Reuss, for soon after he introduced his bill he reported receiving "countless letters from municipal officials, sanitary and hydraulic engineers, conservationists, sportsmen and citizens aggrieved by the growing detergent pollution of our rivers and streams and of ground water."[21]

By March Reuss's bill was before the House Committee on Interstate and Foreign Commerce, but no hearing date had been set. *Chemical and Engineering News* anticipated that the USPHS, in giving its opinion of the bill at any hearing, could easily affect the bill's outcome.[22] If the technical personnel of the USPHS backed the bill, its chances of passing would increase; but if they to opposed it, the reverse would be true. In the meantime the bill was given a fifty-fifty chance of passing that year.

On March 6, 1963, Reuss introduced a substitute bill, H.R. 4571, similar to, but closing a loophole in, H.R. 2105.[23] Although the latter would have banned detergents not meeting decomposability standards from interstate commerce, it would have had no control over intrastate manufacture. So, hard detergents could be sold within the state in which they were manufactured. However, their residues would inevitably end up in interstate waterways, and it was in this connection that the second bill, offered as an amendment to the Federal Water Pollution Control Act, closed the loophole. It would completely ban hard detergents, which could end up in interstate waters. A second significant change was simply to substitute the single word "manufacture" for the words underlined in the following sentence of H.R. 2105 (Section 2): "It shall be unlawful for any person to import into the United States or *introduce or deliver for introduction into interstate commerce* any detergent after June 30, 1965, unless such detergent conforms with standards of decomposability prescribed." Reuss's second bill also followed the West German approach. It required the Secretary of HEW to evolve, in collaboration with industry, standards of degradability within six months of the date of the enactment of the law. (In 1961 Congress had transferred responsibility for the administration of the federal water pollution control program from the Surgeon General to the Secretary of HEW.) After June, 1965, detergents not meeting these standards could neither be marketed in, nor imported into, the United States.

On March 19, 1963, Sen. Lee Metcalf (Democrat, Montana) introduced into the Senate a bill, S. 1118, identical to Reuss's new bill.[24] Within a week a second bill on detergents had been introduced into the Senate by Sen. Maurine B. Neuberger (Democrat, Oregon) for herself and senators Paul H. Douglas (Democrat, Illinois), Edward V. Long (Democrat, Missouri), Warren G. Magnuson (Democrat, Washington), Thomas J. McIntyre (Democrat, New Hampshire), and Gaylord Nelson, until recently the Democratic governor of Wisconsin. While governor, Nelson had learned that almost one-third of the shallow wells in Wisconsin were polluted by detergents. This bill, S. 1183, also utilized Reuss's second bill and consequently was similar to S. 1118.[25] It is noteworthy that Democrats were behind all three bills. Whereas the West German law on detergents called for fines and prison sentences of up to one year for violations, the American bills simply provided for the seizure of any noncomplying detergents and court injunctions against their continued manufacture.

Speaking in support of S. 1183, Senator Nelson explained how studies carried out in Wisconsin had proved that it was "almost impossible" to deal with the detergent pollution problem at the state level.

First of all, it is extremely difficult for a single State to do the research and testing necessary to set standards and impose adequate controls on detergents. Second, it is a principle of physics that water—and the dangerous pollution which stalks our water—does not respect State boundaries. Wisconsin is almost an island, surrounded by rivers and lakes which lead to every part of the Nation. Its underground water supplies follow mysterious underground routes which lead for hundreds of miles.

A determined effort still is being made to enact legislation immediately in Wisconsin to deal with this problem, but even if successful, such legislation cannot guarantee the people of my State that their water will be free of detergent chemical pollution. This can be done only by the U.S. Congress, with a bill such as the one introduced today.[26]

Of the cosponsors of S. 1183, Nelson was its strongest and most knowledgeable proponent. Some of the others displayed serious misconceptions about pollution by detergents, as had Reuss. For instance, in introducing S. 1118 Senator Neuberger stated that "detergents, once finding their way into the water supply, are removed neither by the natural action of bacteria nor the artificial action of water purification plants. And as greater and greater quantities of detergents are discharged into our sewage systems, they remain in the water supply building up at an alarming rate." These views were simply wrong. So also were those of Senator McIntyre, expressed in his maiden speech in the Senate, that "ABS persists for years in ground water," and that it "promotes the growth of undesirable oxygen-demanding algae in streams and of slime obstructions in treatment systems."[27]

It is striking that the two leading proponents of a law to regulate detergents, Reuss and Nelson, were both Democrats from Wisconsin. Other states had also suffered pollution of their groundwaters by detergents, but an environmental consciousness permeated Democratic Wisconsin.[28] A transformed Democratic party became the majority party in the state in 1946 and continued until 1962. The new party was fashioned by William Proxmire, who was elected to the U.S. Senate in 1957. His mentor, John Gaus, a professor of political science at the University of Wisconsin and then at Harvard University, had inspired him to seek "a society within which the life of man was adjusted in the happiest possible manner to the environment in which he lived." Under the Democrats, the state government developed one of the most ambitious conservation programs in the nation.[29] Nelson, a prominent Progressive who had joined the state's new Democratic party, was elected governor in 1958. He established a national reputation as an environmentalist with his advocacy of Wisconsin's Outdoor Recreation Act in 1961.[30] The act provided for fifty million dollars to be spent over the following decade for environmental planning, land acquisition, and a program of easements to preserve scenic values along state highways.

The growing pollution of groundwater by detergents prompted legislative action also at state and county levels in 1963. In April the Dade County (Miami, Florida) Board of Commissioners passed legislation making it unlawful to use, sell, or possess "detergent soaps" after January 1, 1965.[31] In the Maryland legislature a bill had been introduced that would forbid the sale of detergents containing ABS. Furthermore, a joint resolution requested the Maryland governor "to review the need for a standard of degradability in waste treatment systems for detergent materials and to recommend a standard and method for determining such degradability."[32] A third measure introduced in Maryland would forbid, after January 1, 1964, the discharge of untreated detergents from coin-operated laundries and car washing operations into streams and septic tanks. In Reuss and Nelson's home state of Wisconsin one bill had been introduced by March, 1963, which would ban any nondegradable detergent. A second bill was anticipated, which would also outlaw the use of nondegradable detergents and at the same time set up authority for the state board of health to formulate rules and regulations for detergents. Two bills were before the Nebraska legislature. One would place a tax of ten cents per pound on hard detergents, and the other would establish standards of biodegradability and ban detergents not meeting these standards after January 30, 1965. Underlying these bills was the Nebraska Department of Agriculture's plan to produce a degradable detergent based on corn. With the financial support of the department, the Midwest Research Institute had developed a process for making a detergent from cornstarch showing promising biodegradability.[33] Finally, bills in California and Connecticut would also ban the use of nondegradable detergents.

The detergent industry's first public response to these various legislative measures occurred on April 18, 1963, when the board of directors of the Soap and Detergent Association approved the release of a statement by the association's manager, E. Scott Pattison.[34] Pattison called for detergent manufacturers to be allowed to solve the pollution problem through voluntary action. He declared that the proposed legislation could not hasten, and might very well obstruct, the industry's efforts to develop and market more biodegradable products. The industry expected that such products would be available by the end of 1965.

On May 21, 1963, Anthony J. Celebrezze, secretary of HEW, which incorporated the USPHS, issued a report on H.R. 4571. His report recommended deferring legislative action on the bill in order to provide industry the opportunity to reach the proposed voluntary solution of the detergent problem. Celebrezze explained that the industry was currently engaged in efforts to develop a product that would meet the objectives of Reuss's bill, and that it aimed to have completed its work by the end of 1965, only six months after the June 30 deadline set by the bill. His department was ready to work with the industry. "If reasonable progress toward resolving the problem [was] not obtained through such voluntary Government-industry cooperation, we would not hesitate to urge enactment of legislation to accomplish the objectives of H.R. 4571."

Reuss's response was that if a solution could be obtained without legislation he was all for it, but he had some questions.[35] He raised these on June

10 before the Natural Resources and Power Subcommittee of the House Committee on Government Operations, which was holding hearings on water pollution control and abatement. The subcommittee had designated a day for the consideration of detergents. In addition to hearing from Reuss, a member of the House Committee on Government Operations, and Senator Nelson, it also heard from industry representatives. Reuss and Nelson both advocated H.R. 4571 (upon which Nelson and his coauthors had based their S. 1183), although the subcommittee had no jurisdiction over the bill.

Reuss was skeptical about industry's achieving a voluntary agreement that would eliminate the manufacture or marketing of hard detergents by all companies. Some observers had speculated that a decision to abandon the use of ABS by one or more large users, including Procter and Gamble, Lever Brothers, and Colgate-Palmolive, would cause ABS to decline in price. Reuss wondered if such an outcome would then encourage the continued, or even expanded, use of ABS by companies that did not participate in the agreement. If so, responsible companies would then find themselves at a financial disadvantage relative to their irresponsible competitors. In West Germany, efforts to obtain a voluntary agreement had apparently foundered when some industries refused to cooperate. There, said Reuss, it had proved necessary to resort to legislation, not only to further the national goal of purer water, but also to protect the cooperative and responsible companies from unfair, unscrupulous competition. Furthermore, no agreement made among American companies would affect foreign producers. How, asked Reuss, would it be possible to prevent a large importation of hard detergents, especially if there were a price differential between hard detergents and the new degradable detergents being offered by American companies?

The six months difference between the effective date of H.R. 4571 and the date aimed at by industry did not appear to Reuss to be of crucial significance, provided the industry intended a complete switch to soft detergents. However, if the industry intended only to begin marketing such detergents at the end of 1965, while still selling hard detergents, that was a very different proposition, for detergent pollution would then continue.

Reuss also asked whether the industry was willing to make a binding agreement. "It will not serve the public interest or indeed the long run interests of industry to create the illusion that means of ending detergent pollution have been found and then to discover, in the moment of truth, that 'unforeseen difficulties' prevent the conversion to degradable detergents." An additional question was whether states or localities would consider a voluntary agreement by industry sufficient. If not, they could, as some were already doing, impose their own regulations. "We could end up with a patchwork of local and State ordinances that would impede interstate commerce and hurt the economy by balkanizing the detergent market."[36]

Despite these concerns, Reuss was willing to go along with a voluntary approach under a schedule that would leave time to protect the public interest if it proved impossible to implement an effective, voluntary agreement. He challenged the industry to begin immediate negotiations with HEW to work out a timely and effective agreement. Hearings were to be held on H.R. 4571 shortly after August 1, and Reuss urged representatives of HEW and the detergent industry to be ready then to present a draft agreement to end detergent pollution and to answer the questions he had raised. If an agreement were not possible he would then expect HEW to recommend, as Celebrezze had urged in his letter of May 21, "the enactment of legislation to accomplish the objectives of H.R. 4571." Nelson, however, believed that a solution would "never come voluntarily," because the industry's attitude was that water pollution by detergents was only a small part of the overall water pollution problem. But his own attitude was that "we have to start someplace. This is a feasible place to start."[37]

The holding of hearings meant, of course, that the industry would present its position publicly. Colgate-Palmolive had privately indicated to Reuss their general support of H.R. 4571, and he had hailed them in the House on May 13 for "their public spirited position."[38] Now a team of six representatives of industry led by David C. Melnicoff, president of Fels and Company and president of the Soap and Detergent Association at the time, gave testimony. In view of the association's thorough investigation of the detergent pollution problem, considered in chapter 3, the representatives must have felt secure in their knowledge. Charles Bueltman, a sanitary engineer and the association's technical director, stated that ABS had no adverse effects on sewage treatment techniques. He said, in a frequently repeated remark that would not fail to irritate Reuss and Nelson, that ABS had "been looked to as a useful tool for improving the quality of sewage treatment plant effluents."[39] The general idea was, as indicated in an earlier chapter, that where there was foam there must also be other, and more dangerous, pollutants from sewage, which might otherwise go undetected. For example, when considering polluted groundwater and the resulting foam in a glass of drinking water, some regarded ABS as playing a positive role in alerting consumers to more serious contamination. However, Nelson would soon respond that the presence of ABS did not necessarily imply the presence of other pollutants, nor its absence their absence. Bueltman also stated that ABS had had no detrimental effects on water treatment techniques and that the levels of ABS in potable waters were well below the USPHS recommended maximum of half a milligram of ABS per liter. Nevertheless, he admitted that in "a few special situations" there were problems with ABS. However, he assured the committee that the industry had voluntarily assumed the responsibility of removing the residues of their products, even in these "isolated situations."[40]

Frank J. Coughlin, associate director of product development for the soap products division of Procter and Gamble and a former chairman of the Soap and Detergent Association's Research Steering Committee, testified next regarding possible effects on human health from consumption of trace amounts of ABS in drinking water supplies. He made two principal points. First, the preponderance of extensive scientific evidence clearly and incontrovertibly proved that the current levels of ABS in drinking water supplies were not harmful to humans and could not, in any sense, be categorized as a health hazard. Second, numerous studies also fully supported the conclusion that there was no long-term health hazard—no cumulative ill effect—from prolonged ingestion of the minute trace amounts of ABS normally found in the nation's drinking water supplies. Coughlin was aware of the argument that a given substance cannot be proved safe until it has been tested on successive generations of man himself. But it seemed both to him and the industry that such an argument did not properly take into account the entire body of scientific procedures and knowledge. Scientific studies involving animals, he said, provided reasonably accurate predictions of effects on humans.[41]

Dr. Richard B. Wearn, a director of research for Colgate-Palmolive and vice chairman of the technical and materials research committee of the Soap and Detergent Association, gave an account of the research carried out within the industry and that sponsored by the association. Acknowledging that foaming in water supplies and in streams was "objectionable," he continued that the industry was determined to remove ABS from its products as soon as it was feasible to do so, and thus eliminate any foaming to which ABS contributed. To this end, he said, the manufacturers of household detergents and the suppliers of the principal raw materials were individually busily engaged in research to find readily decomposable surfactants to substitute for ABS. He reported that Colgate-Palmolive had a very promising detergent, which he did not specify, in the final testing stage. Although he could not speak with specific knowledge about other manufacturers, it appeared that they had made similar progress to Colgate-Palmolive.[42]

Henry Moss, an industrial chemist with Monsanto Chemical Company and a past chairman of the Technical Advisory Council and Research Steering Committee of the Soap and Detergent Association, next discussed, from the perspective of a supplier of raw materials to the detergent industry, the activities directed to the development of more readily biodegradable surfactants during the preceding several years. He quoted Monsanto's vice president to the effect that the company intended to convert completely to a new, more biodegradable product in 1965. The final member of the industrial team, John Moser, vice president of Lever Brothers Company and vice chairman of the Technical and Materials Division of the Soap and Detergent Association, added that the industry could place new detergents on the market within about ten months after satisfactory formulas had been established in the laboratory and after sizeable quantities of new detergent base became available.[43] In concluding the formal presentations, Melnicoff quoted from the April 18 statement of E. Scott Pattison, manager of the Soap and Detergent Association, to the effect that individual companies would be producing the more degradable products "by the end of 1965." He added, "As a matter of corporate and industrial self-interest as well as good responsible citizenship, we are hard at work improving our products so that both the users of our products and those concerned with water resources will both be well served."[44]

Rep. Robert McClory (Republican, Illinois), an incisive member of the Natural Resources and Power Subcommittee of the House Committee on Government Operations and one sympathetic to the industry, felt that the "most serious testimony" presented had been that hard detergents did not break down but instead traveled long distances in the ground and penetrated underground water supplies. He wondered what effect, if any, the new soft detergents would have in reducing pollution from existing septic tanks.[45] In reply, Bueltman referred to field experiments being conducted at the time on the new materials by the association in cooperation with New York state's Temporary Water Resources Committee on Long Island. Some thirty to thirty-five sampling wells had been drilled in an effort to determine what the effect might be, but the study was still unfinished.

The first public hearing at the federal level on pollution by detergents had provided legislators with an overview of the problem's history and a statement on its current status. The widely used ABS was seen not to be a hazard either to human or aquatic life in the concentrations in which it was found in various waters; but the foam produced by ABS was considered a nuisance, aesthetically undesirable wherever it occurred, and expensive to remove in sewage treatment plants. The detergent industry, which had actively been seeking a satisfactory substitute for ABS, reiterated its intention of producing such by the end of 1965.

Just over two weeks later a second team of industrial representatives—including some members of the earlier team, led this time by E. Scott Pattison—testified on June 26, 1963. They came before the recently created Special Subcommittee on Air and Water Pollution of the Senate Committee on Public Works holding hearings on the two detergent bills, S. 1118 and S. 1183, and also on S. 649. This last bill, which had been introduced on January 1, 1963, by Sen. Edmund Muskie (Democrat, Maine), chairman of the subcommittee, also sought to amend the Federal Water Pollution Control Act. During the early 1960s various members of Congress had expressed dissatisfaction with the slow pace of water pollution control.[46] They criticized states for not doing as much as they could, and the Public Health Service, responsible for administering the Water Pollution Control Act, as being either unwilling or unable to make states do more. Muskie's bill embraced a set of far-reaching amendments to the Water Pollution Control Act. Under these, administrative authority for the act would be transferred to a new federal water pollution control administration to be created within HEW; federal and state enforcement would be based on water quality standards for interstate waters; and these standards could be set by the Secretary of HEW if the secretary judged standards set by states to be inadequate. A week prior to the industry's appearance, Nelson and Neuberger had testified before the subcommittee, of which Nelson was a member.

The thrust of Pattison's remarks was to oppose legislation and support voluntary action by the industry, and he began by noting that the industry's position was not out of harmony with that stated by HEW's Secretary Celebrezze on May 21 in regard to Reuss's H.R. 4571. He also noted that even Reuss had said, "I believe in voluntary cooperation over legislation any time it will work and I am certainly willing to try."[47] To the industry it seemed that four points deserved particular consideration, and it would appear that here they had in mind Reuss's earlier questions. First, were the dimensions of the detergent problem either so general, so severe, or so perilous that correction of the problem could not be left to the industry under its declared schedule? Pattison argued that if the residues of detergents currently in use were indeed creating a public health hazard, then there should be no delay in removing them from the market. However, at the concentrations found in water supplies ABS had no toxic effects, and its presence in sewage did not significantly interfere with the normal biological processes of sewage treatment.[48] Regarding foam caused by ABS in sewage plant aeration tanks, Pattison observed: "we have a nuisance problem here—an esthetic problem—with a high visibility factor that is creating a public reaction against our products. Thus, our first job has been to find product improvements that will get us out and away from the overall water pollution complex."[49] To attempt to downplay the problem by characterizing it as an aesthetic one was hardly persuasive at a time of incipient national concern for natural beauty.[50]

The second consideration was whether there was a serious likelihood of noncompliance—by manufacturers other than those representing some 90 percent of the industry's business who had made commitments to comply— and whether the public needed, or the industry wanted, protection from possible noncompliers. Here Pattison stated that there were in the United States "a relatively few—five or six—producers" of ABS. Without the demand from a similarly small number of large detergent producers, ABS would be "technically obsolescent" and consequently "no bargain for anybody." The possible importation of ABS into the United States seemed equally unrealistic, "since a tariff of 25 percent ad valorem, plus 3.5 cents per pound, on top of transportation costs, is far more than any differential between the older and the improved product which is likely to exist, even temporarily."[51]

The third point was whether in regard to biodegradability the industry would improve its products enough to abate the objectionable effects ascribed to them. Pattison had been assured that products proposed for use in the United States would more than meet the legislated German standard for biodegradability.[52]

The final consideration was why the industry objected to future regulation even if enforcement was so postdated that it would merely confirm and assure the industry's voluntary commitments. Here Pattison made two points. First, any effort to impose at some future date a specific legal standard of biodegradability seemed to the industry likely to slow down improvement until the standard was fully defined. The main objective then would be simply to comply, rather than to apply flexibility and creativeness to ending the existing problems. Second, there would then be a legal requirement that every product of every producer or converter, national or local, would be subjected to a complicated test routine.[53]

Of the various industrial representatives testifying, J. Gibson Pleasants, vice president for research and development at Procter and Gamble, seems to have had thought most deeply about the industry's position in regard to developing a substitute for ABS. Certainly he was the most articulate representative. Having suggested in his prepared statement that the industry and the subcommittee were in agreement that the detergent problem must be resolved, he claimed that he had reached that conclusion perhaps well before anyone in government. Had he not so concluded, he continued, he would have been derelict in his duty, for he would have failed to carry out a managerial responsibility that demanded a recognition of what was right in the public interest as well as what was in his company's interest. As for his fellow managers at Procter and Gamble, they had been convinced that the problem had to be solved before it became the subject of much discussion within government. That government and industry were in agreement meant to Pleasants that "the problem is now well over half solved, and, moreover, will definitely be solved."[54] He firmly believed that the current situation—where the proposed legislation carried an implicit warning that the government might decide to give detergent industry management some rather precise managerial instructions—was not one that encouraged a recalcitrant attitude on the part of managers and owners. Pleasants could not envision a detergent company risking legislative and public wrath and tremendous competitive pressures, when the industry, through its association, had stated that the problem must and would be solved. He assured the legislators that "a tremendous revolution" was taking place in the detergent industry, that the goal was in sight and attainable on schedule. The industry, he said, could not see how legislation could further the revolution. To the contrary, it was convinced that legislation would impede what otherwise would be rapid progress.

In response to a question from Senator Muskie probing the industry's opposition to legislation, Pleasants elaborated upon his own stance. He explained how one school of thought held that "the less statutory government we have, the less problem we have," while a second held the contrasting view that "things are simply tidier if they are well covered by legislation." [55] Pleasants belonged to the former school "by instinct, by background;" he took pride in voluntary accomplishment and favored the least possible government. In the current situation the progress being made by the detergent industry strengthened his opposition to the proposed legislation, which he characterized as "a possibly disruptive and offensive method of compulsion." This response satisfied Muskie, and no industrial representative added to it.

Overall, the industry had presented its case tellingly. The general impression it created was that satisfactory new detergents were well on their way to development in time to meet the deadline of December 31, 1965, and therefore legislation was not needed. The industry readily acceded to the request of Sen. Jack R. Miller (Republican, Iowa)—that it furnish the subcommittee with status reports on the development of the new detergents every six months beginning on September 30, 1964—indicating an inclination to support a voluntary solution. [56]

While Congress had been considering the proposed legislation on detergents, so too had a task group of the American Water Works Association. The group noted that at one time some had thought that the British might be the first to enact restrictive legislation, but thus far they had not seen fit to do so. To the contrary, the 1962 report of the British Standing Technical Committee on Synthetic Detergents had rejected the idea of restrictions because of satisfactory progress made by the British detergent industry and belief that further progress toward a softer detergent would be retarded were restrictions imposed. [57]

The task group added that although anyone interested in water conservation could scarcely do anything but praise legislation designed to protect water quality, nevertheless it found deficiencies in the proposed federal legislation. First, the objectives of the bills were quite limited, as the relationship of detergents to water quality was a part, but only a part, of the overall problem of maintaining the quality of natural waters. Second, the bills as written seemed to apply to all cleaning products containing surface active agents and not merely to domestic and industrial detergents. Since there were hundreds of the former, the task group believed that if the bills were enacted, administration of the law would require an unreasonable amount of routine testing by the USPHS—a point, it will be recalled, also made by Pattison.

Even if the bills were corrected in this respect, developing standards for bio-degradability and testing domestic and industrial detergents would be major undertakings. The creation and maintenance of such a program would require Congress to appropriate substantial sums of money each year. The task group felt that the money and scientific talent that would be devoted to testing could probably be used to better advantage in dealing with other aspects of water pollution and its control. Because of these perceived deficiencies, and be-cause responsible representatives of the detergent industry had made assur-ances that the entire industry would be converting to soft detergents by the end of 1965, the task group concluded that the American Water Works As-sociation should not support the proposed legislation "*at this time.*" Indeed, "the Association should point out the limitations, the probable administrative difficulties, the expense of the proposed legislation, and the apparent lack of need for such a law in view of progress by the detergent industry toward the same goal." Only one member of the group dissented, filing a minority re-port.[58] The association's board of directors subsequently accepted the group's recommendation and decided during the summer of 1963 neither to support nor fight the proposed federal legislation.[59]

When S. 649 was reported out of the Committee on Public Works in early October, 1963, it had been amended to include a section on detergents reflect-ing the concerns of S. 1183 and S. 1118. Although the committee did not believe that legislation prohibiting the production and sale of hard detergents was necessary at that time, nevertheless it felt that some procedural legisla-tion might be advisable in order to ensure an expeditious solution to the de-tergent problem.[60] Consequently, it provided for the detergent industry and HEW to undertake a cooperative venture towards solving the problem.

The bill authorized appointing a technical committee made up of equal numbers of representatives from HEW and the detergent industry. The com-mittee would serve in a liaison capacity to evaluate progress in the develop-ment of acceptable decomposable detergents and to recommend the standards of decomposability to be met by them. On or before January 1, 1965, and again on June 30, 1965, the Secretary of HEW was to report to Congress any measures taken toward the resolution of the detergent pollution problem, the nature of any delays encountered, and his recommendations for additional legislation, if necessary, to regulate the composition of detergents transported or sold in interstate commerce.

After the committee would have recommended standards of decomposa-bility, and certified to the secretary that materials conforming to desirable standards of decomposability were generally available to manufacturers of detergents, the secretary might, if he concurred in the findings of the com-mittee, establish such rules and regulations as were necessary to prevent the transportation or sale in interstate commerce of detergents not meeting the standards of decomposability. He was also required, in conjunction with the Secretary of the Treasury, to issue rules and regulations preventing the importation of detergents not meeting the standards of decomposability. These regulations would take effect on December 31, 1965, or six months after the issuance of such regulations, whichever was later.

When on October 16, 1963, the Senate debated S. 649 as amended, Senator Nelson, confining his remarks to pollution of water by detergents, explained why he believed legislation was needed. He read from a letter, which he had received on August 22, 1963, from E. Scott Pattison, manager of the Soap and Detergent Association. "I can assure you that those producers of synthetic detergents and their suppliers who are members of this association have indeed definitely stated their intention to make a changeover in composition. There is every reason to believe that this changeover to more biodegradable surfactants will have taken place prior to December 31, 1965, based on the present outlook for adequate supplies of the new materials."[61] Nelson, however, considered the industry's promise insufficient. First, he regarded it as being so heavily qualified as to be almost meaningless. The industry had "never specified a deadline by which a changeover to safe detergents by all producers will have been completed." Second, no standards were set; Nelson asked rhetorically what good a changeover to a new product was if its characteristics were unknown. Third, no enforcement or supervisory procedure was proposed. Nelson accused the industry of wanting "to correct a threat to the public at its own convenience, according to its own standards, and with no machinery for determining whether it has carried out its promise." Fourth, Nelson believed there was reason to question the good faith, or at least the consistency and sincerity, with which the industry had faced up to the detergent pollution problem. He accused the industry of having spread the "completely false" notions that among the many kinds of pollution deriving from sewage, detergent pollution was a minor one; and that since detergent pollution was visible—because of foaming—it served as a valuable warning or a "tracer" of other and more dangerous forms of pollution.

Nelson was convinced that progress toward eliminating pollution by detergents, "this threat to the public," had come from one principal source, namely, legislative pressure. He noted that the industry had made its much-advertised decision to change over to soft detergents by December 31, 1965, on April 18, 1963, some three weeks after he and Senators Neuberger and McIntyre had introduced their joint bill. Then the industry had first made its decision public at a hearing before a committee of the Wisconsin legislature considering a bill to ban hard detergents after June 30, 1965. The facts, concluded Nelson, "show that all the promises of the industry were made long after the problem was well known, and were made only to delay or avoid legislation which would correct the problem."

On October 16, 1963, S. 649 was passed by the Senate, sixty-nine to eleven with twenty abstentions.[62] On the following day it was referred to the House Committee on Public Works, which held hearings on it, on Reuss's H.R. 4571, and on two related bills in early December, 1963, and, following the Christmas recess, in February, 1964. During this period Wisconsin became the first state in the nation to ban the sale of nondegradable household detergents. On December 18 Gov. John W. Reynolds signed into law a bill making the ban effective from December 31, 1965, and requiring detergent manufacturers in the meanwhile to report periodically to the state's board of health on the progress being made towards marketing soft detergents.[63]

At the hearings before the Committee on Public Works a third industrial contingent testified, whose leader was David Melnicoff, president of the Soap and Detergent Association and of Fels-Naptha Company of Philadelphia. He declared at the outset that the contingent's objective was to oppose section twelve of S. 649, the section dealing with synthetic detergents, as being unnecessary. Melnicoff hoped that the House committee would agree that the best way to resolve problems arising out of industrial practices was by voluntary effort and cooperation with government agencies. If the creation of new legislation and its attendant regulatory paraphernalia could be avoided, it would be wise to do so. Such a course would not deny the vital interest of government in the pollution problem, and it would allow for maximum flexibility and for creative action, both important in a field in which much was yet unknown and in which technology was constantly changing. Section twelve of S. 649 called for a joint committee of industry and HEW to establish a standard of biodegradability; but, said Melnicoff, the two were already jointly developing a test method on which to base such a standard.[64]

Of greater significance, Melnicoff announced that the industry was well on its way to producing a replacement for ABS. For the first time, the public heard of LAS, linear alkyl sulfonate. Charles E. Bueltman, technical director of the Soap and Detergent Association, provided a demonstration of how completely LAS was degraded by the sewage treatment process. Paul E. Geiser, general manager of petrochemical operations for the Continental Oil Company, which had been a major supplier of ABS since 1948, described the progress Continental Oil and the industry as a whole had been making towards the new product. He expressed the industry's confidence that sufficient LAS would be available by the end of 1965 to meet the entire domestic demand. E. Scott Pattison, manager of the Soap and Detergent Association, submitted letters from all suppliers in support of Geiser's statement.[65] Detergent producers also supported it. John Halsted, vice president of the Colgate-Palmolive Company, stated that his company estimated that by the end of 1965 all stocks of "nonbiodegradable" detergents would be used up and that dealers, wholesalers, and retailers would be completely supplied with "biodegradable" detergents. Likewise the Purex Corporation was planning for "100-percent conversion to biodegradable types of detergent alkanes during 1965."[66] J. Gibson Pleasants of the Procter and Gamble Company reported a more optimistic view: "unless some presently unforeseen difficulties should develop as we move to full plant operation, we expect that we shall be able to beat the Soap and Detergent Association's December 31, 1965, target date by several months."[67]

The chairman of the House Committee on Public Works was John Blatnik (Democrat-Farmer-Labor, Minnesota), an author of the Federal Water Pollution Control Act of 1956 and chief architect in the House of the important 1961 amendments to it. He was most impressed by the industry's performance, calling it "the best organized and the best conducted presentation that I have witnessed, observed, in [the] 17 years I have been on this committee."[68] The industry had done its utmost to make section twelve of S. 649 seem quite unnecessary, and had at least made a great impression on the committee's chairman.

Reuss had followed the industry's testimony with interest and had concluded that it marked "great" progress. "For the first time they stated publicly and unanimously that nondegradable detergents, both domestic and imported, will not be used in this country after December 1965. This is real progress and the industry should be commended for it." However, Reuss insisted that standards and simple legislation were still necessary and that the Secretary of HEW was the public official who alone, in the final analysis, could set those standards. In this connection Reuss suggested an amendment to section twelve of S. 649 (section twelve provided for a technical committee composed of equal numbers of representatives from the industry and HEW). Reuss argued that under this arrangement, should the industry disagree with the public representatives as to standards, or as to keeping noncomplying detergents out of interstate commerce, they would in effect have a veto power. So he suggested "that while there would be a technical committee composed equally of public and industry representatives, and while the Secretary would be obligated to consult with them, the actual public determination of standards would be made by the Secretary, and it also would be up to the Secretary to, on his own initiative, assign a cutoff date."[69]

When the Committee on Public Works resumed its hearings after the Christmas recess, a most important statement was made on February 5, 1964, by LeRoy H. Hurlbert, vice president and general counsel of the Colgate-Palmolive Company.[70] He reported on a field test of Colgate-Palmolive's new detergents based on LAS. The test was conducted jointly by a team from Colgate-Palmolive and one from the Johns Hopkins University. The former was led by Richard B. Wearn, director of research for the company, and the latter by Prof. Charles E. Renn, who was currently serving as chairman of the governor of Maryland's special committee on detergent degradability.

The test site at the Elm Farm Mobile Homes Park near Woodbridge, Virginia, had an efficient, modern sewage treatment plant. The ninety-six resident families all agreed to use only the test products—Dynamo, Fab, Ad, Ajax Cleanser, Ajax All-Purpose Cleaner, Liquid Vel, and Soaky—issued free at the Park's grocery store, in lieu of the detergents normally used. As the tests progressed the rapid decrease in detergent concentration in the sewage treatment plant effluent was accompanied by a "spectacular" reduction within the sewage plant itself. When the test began, the concentration of ABS in the sewage effluent was about 8 ppm; between the tenth and the fifteenth weeks of the tests, the concentration of LAS in the effluent fell to 0.5 ppm and leveled out at that figure. Furthermore, over 80 percent of the housewives at Elm Farm considered the test products as good as or better than any of the products they had used hitherto.

In concluding, Hurlbert read into the record a telling statement by James M. Quigley, Assistant Secretary of HEW. "These tests, carried out on a full plant scale, afford proof that the new detergents, when subjected to efficient sewage treatment practices currently in use, can be degraded to a level which eliminates detergent foam. When these and similar new detergents come into general use within the next year, a solution to one of urban America's most amazing pollution problems will have been effected."[71] To date there was no adequate data on the degradability of the new LAS-based products in cesspools, septic tanks, and similar facilities, but the industry was working toward that end.

The Committee on Public Works was much impressed by Hurlbert's statement. Said Rep. Robert T. McLoskey (Republican, Illinois): "Whether it is because of the threat of legislation or for what[ever] the reason, industry itself does recognize the problem and they are taking steps to correct it. And am I not right that, in view of this, this situation can be handled through private— through industry without action from the Federal Government?" Hurlbert replied, "That is our position and our belief."[72]

When the Committee on Public Works reported in early September, 1964, it had removed the proposed new section twelve to the Federal Water Pollution Control Act, which would have provided for the promulgation of standards of decomposability for synthetic detergents.[73] The report explained that a convincing demonstration had been made by industry that the problem of indecomposability of detergents had been under attack for some time and that "the solution is either already at hand or will be at hand in the near future." The industry was developing a new and improved product under a self-imposed deadline well in advance of that specified in the bill. The report added that should "any lack of progress toward this objective indicate that regulatory legislation is necessary the committee will at that time promptly consider the need and the advisability of enactment of such controls."[74] The committee was serious about strengthening water pollution control, for it adopted in general Muskie's proposals.[75] The industry had gotten what it wanted; now it had to meet its promised deadline.

In tackling the detergent pollution problem at the level of public concern, Representative Reuss and Senator Nelson, both of Wisconsin, tried to have the United States follow the West German rather than the British example, but they had no success. The detergent pollution problem was much less severe in the United States than in either Germany or Britain, and for that reason it took longer to be raised at the national government level. By the time bills were introduced into the U.S. Congress, the international detergent industry had been working on a solution to the detergent pollution problem for several years and had made considerable progress.

Principally because of this progress, but also for philosophical reasons, the industry's appeal for a voluntary solution to the problem was favored over legislation. Students of comparative national public policy have noted "basic differences in inherited attitudes toward governmental initiatives and intervention. On the one hand British and American traditions favor limits on government power, as is reflected both in individualist values and in the sharp borders perceived between private and public spheres. By contrast, in Sweden, France, the Netherlands, and Germany, traditions allow governments more freedom to devise innovative solutions for problems caused by industrialization, urbanization, and other facets of socio-economic development."[76] Clearly the American and British and the contrasting West German ways of tackling the problem of pollution by synthetic detergents fit these generalizations.

VI

Fashioning an Acceptable Surfactant

During its extended search for a substitute for ABS, the American detergent industry avidly monitored the corresponding searches of its counterparts in Britain and West Germany. It profited by doing so; but the way to a fully satisfactory surfactant, LAS (linear alkyl sulfonate), was finally opened following the development of molecular sieve technology in the United States during 1962–63.

From the mid-1950s the United States detergent industry had sought a substitute for ABS, and by 1963 it had synthesized and tested over 750 compounds.[1] Obviously it was no easy task to find a replacement for ABS, an isomeric mixture, which over the years had been developed into an outstanding product in all respects, except for the resistance of some of its isomers to biodegradation. In order to be successful in the high-volume household detergent market, a surfactant had to possess a unique combination of properties, including high cleaning performance, safety, no or low toxicity, acceptable color and odor, and, of course, availability in the hundreds of millions of pounds used annually. To this list had now been added the requirement of rapid and complete biodegradability.

The unsatisfactory degree of biodegradation of ABS was attributed to the branched-chain nature of some of its isomers. In contrast, surfactants derived from straight-chain fatty acids were known to biodegrade readily. So it seemed plausible that a straight-chain alkyl benzene sulfonate might degrade readily.[2] One of the promising laboratory creations first tested in the United States in 1956 was a straight-chain product later to be known as linear alkyl sulfonate (LAS).[3] But it remained a laboratory curiosity at the time, as no practical method of producing large quantities of it was known. ABS, as noted in chapter one, was produced from an inexpensive branched-chain hydrocarbon readily available from petroleum refineries, but no economical means of obtaining a straight-chain hydrocarbon existed.

By 1958, it will be recalled, the British had developed Dobane JN, a straight-chain alkylate.[4] It was derived from the cracking of petroleum wax, an approach that attracted considerable interest in the United States. In this process, as eventually conducted in the United States, selected petroleum waxes were heated to about $1,000°$ F in the presence of steam or nitrogen as a dilutent at a pressure under 100 pounds per square inch and with a contact time of less than thirty seconds. Under these conditions, conversion of the wax to olefins with twenty carbon atoms or fewer was of the order of 80 percent, of which the alpha-olefin content was about 95 percent.[5] From the alpha-olefins a variety of readily degradable surfactants could be manufactured.[6]

From the beginning, however, it was apparent that the wax-cracking route to a more satisfactory surfactant had serious drawbacks. The Monsanto Chemical Company, one of the major suppliers of alkylate in the United States, calculated that producing the required 400 million pounds of olefin by cracking wax (to replace the quantity of tetrapropylene being used annually by 1963) would result in the production of 1.6 billion pounds of useless residues.[7] Furthermore, the two billion pounds of petroleum wax required to do this were simply not available in 1963, even if all other existing uses of petroleum wax were to be discontinued.

Another drawback in deriving olefins from the cracking of wax was expense. In the highly competitive detergent industry, American companies watched closely what was happening abroad. In West Germany, Chemische Werke Huels, the country's largest synthetic detergent manufacturer, had also been looking for a substitute for ABS since 1956 and had considered alpha-olefins. However, on March 18, 1963, *Chemical and Engineering News* reported that Huels had concluded that olefins were too expensive.[8]

In West Germany, Rheinpreussen A. G. fur Bergbau und Chemie had studied ABS chain length in regard to speed of degradation.[9] Results indicated that the C_{10} to C_{13} isomers degraded most rapidly. In the Ziegler polymerization of ethylene only about 50 percent by weight of the alpha-olefins produced were ten-, twelve-, and fourteen-carbon-atom olefins.[10] Nevertheless, this was a higher percentage than that obtained with the wax-cracking process, in which only about 25 percent by weight of the olefins produced were in the C_{10} to C_{14} range. Here was yet another drawback to cracking wax.

In early 1963, about the time that Congressman Reuss was introducing his detergent bills in Congress, the alpha-olefin route to a new detergent appeared to be preferred in the United States, with eight companies building plants to produce these olefins. The cost of olefins was still in question, but as *Chemical and Engineering News* observed, "Price may not be a factor—if legislation forces a switch to new materials."[11]

About the same time, West Germany's Chemische Werke Huels announced a pilot plant producing straight-chain paraffins in the C_{12} to C_{14} range as a new material for detergents. Huels expected to begin full-scale production in about a year, and anticipated that the cost of the new surfactant based on normal-paraffins would be only slightly higher than that of ABS.[12] In producing straight-chain paraffins, Huels was exploiting the new technology of molecular sieves destined to be central to the large-scale production of a more completely biodegradable surfactant.

Of the six companies supplying detergent alkylate in the United States in the early 1960s, Continental Oil was in second place, supplying 150 million of the combined 500 million pounds annual production.[13] In keeping abreast of new developments, the company had constructed a plant for the production of alpha-olefins. But on May 15, 1963, Continental's board of directors approved a capital expenditure of some seven million dollars for the construction of new, and conversion of existing, facilities to produce straight-chain paraffins. These new intermediates, to be sold under Continental's tradename Nalkylene, were to be available from September, 1964. On the heels of Continental Oil's decision, Union Carbide, which had not hitherto been in the detergent alkylate supply business, also decided to produce paraffin intermediates.[14] Carbide would start with paraffin crude and separate normal- from iso-paraffins using a molecular sieve process developed by its Linde Company division.

By early November of 1963, it seemed to *Chemical and Engineering News* that normal-paraffins were holding the inside track as the material that would replace propylene tetramer to make "a biologically soft alkylbenzene."[15] And in May of 1964 *Chemical Week* reported that interest in alpha-olefins as starting materials for surfactants had "dropped sharply" during the preceding year. A comparison of projected costs indicated that normal-paraffins would yield a cheaper product than alpha-olefins. Two alkylate manufacturers already using the cracked wax route were scheduled to replace it with the normal-paraffin route in 1965. The latter became the principal route to the new surfactant LAS.[16]

Naturally occurring molecular sieves had been known since the 1920s when the crystalline zeolites, which are hydrated alumino-silicate minerals, were observed to have remarkable adsorption properties after activation by dehydration.[17] It was found that dehydrated crystalline zeolites enabled molecules to be separated on the basis of size. Due to scarcity of crystalline zeolites, however, their properties could not be exploited commercially before the early 1950s, when synthetic crystalline zeolites were first developed by the Linde Company, a division, as noted, of the Union Carbide Corporation. Molecular sieve technology had then been used in the petroleum industry.[18] However, the sieving of C_{10} to C_{15} fractions, which presented major problems compared with lighter fractions, was a development triggered entirely by the need for softer surfactants.[19] It was the key development on the road to a satisfactory substitute for ABS and occurred during 1962–63.

The first public mention of molecular sieves in relation to the detergent industry appeared in *Chemical and Engineering News* on October 29, 1962. This was some three months before Reuss introduced his first bill. In reporting that Union Carbide Olefins might move into the alpha-olefin market shortly, the journal stated, "Apparently, Carbide would get at alpha-olefins through vapor phase separation of paraffins, using molecular sieves." This point was repeated by the journal on March 18, 1963. Furthermore, at the same time it also reported that the Phillips Company might employ a molecular sieve extraction of kerosene to get a straight-chain paraffin.[20] The company would then use the chlorination-alkylation route to a straight-chain alkylbenzene. Also on the same page the journal added that Chemische Werke Huels had decided to use straight-chain paraffins in the C_{12} to C_{14} range as a raw material. Huels would buy the paraffins from Gelesenberg-Benzin, which had licensed the molecular sieve process called Molex developed by the Universal Oil Products Company of Des Plaines, Illinois, to produce them. "In searching for suitable raw materials which would be economically available, Gelesenberg-Benzin said that tests conducted by Huels Chemical Works on the sample product from the UOP Molex process proved so excellent that Gelesenberg-Benzin had decided to license and build the first commercial Molex unit."[21]

Regarding the nature of the molecular sieve process, when the water of hydration is removed from crystalline zeolites by heating, the crystal structure remains unchanged, leaving an empty but uniformly porous network.[22] This porous structure has an affinity for molecules of a definite size and shape. In the separation of normal-paraffins from kerosene, for example, molecular sieves with pore diameters of 5 angstroms were used. The normal-paraffins, which have cross-sectional diameters of 4.9 angstroms, are readily adsorbed, while branched compounds, napthenes, and aromatics are rejected because of their larger cross-sectional diameters.

A separation of normal-paraffins could also be accomplished by complexing with urea, which the British had used to obtain olefins for the production of Dobane JNO 36.[23] Urea complexes and molecular sieves are members of a group of adsorption materials called inclusion compounds. The urea complexes are so-called "canal" complexes arising from adsorption within separate tubular cavities inside crystal lattices. The canal diameters are about 5 angstroms, appropriate for accommodation of normal-paraffin molecules.

Molecular sieves could be utilized in several processes, each involving a different adsorption and desorption cycle.[24] One process employed the pressure-swing cycle, in which adsorption occurred at one pressure and desorption at a lower pressure. A second employed the thermal-swing cycle, which utilized a given temperature for adsorption and a higher one for desorption. A third used the purge-gas stripping cycle, which involved purging the sieve with a non-adsorbable gas, causing desorption by lowering the partial pressure of the adsorbate in the vapor phase. A final process was based on the displacement cycle, which employed an adsorbable fluid that displaced all or part of previously adsorbed material.

By late 1964 three commercial sieve processes had been developed in the United States and were either in use or slated for use. Union Carbide's Olefins Division used the IsoSiv process developed by Carbide and employing a vapor phase pressure-swing cycle. Normal-paraffins were adsorbed from the vapor phase at moderate to atmospheric pressures, and then recovered from the sieve by reducing the pressure to 10–250 millimeters of mercury. Universal Oil Products' Molex process employed a liquid-phase displacement cycle. In this process paraffins were recovered by flooding the spent sieve with paraffins of lower molecular weight; the lower and higher paraffins in the resulting mixture were then separated by distillation.[25] Esso's sieve process employed a vapor thermal-swing cycle. Vaporized kerosene was fed to the sieve at about atmospheric pressure, and desorption was accomplished by employing a higher temperature than that used in adsorption. Shell was apparently the only company using the urea complex method for separating normal-paraffins from petroleum stocks. It would appear then that the potential of the adsorption route to a new surfactant had been recognized simultaneously by several parties and that laboratory success was experienced from 1962. Two years later the route had been developed to the production level.[26]

Although the detergent industry had mounted a cooperative effort in studying the pollution problem, when it came to producing surfactants for the new detergents and the detergents themselves, individual companies worked alone in secrecy for their share of the lucrative detergent market. Information on their activities is sparse, but as suppliers of raw materials presumably proceeded along broadly similar lines, an outline of Monsanto's activities, presented at a Senate hearing, should illustrate the general approach.[27] Research on the development of more readily biodegradable surfactants was initiated within Monsanto as early as 1956, and by June of 1963 the company had spent roughly three million dollars on research. By the latter date work on biodegradable detergents was the most extensive single research activity within Monsanto, involving forty-two full-time technical specialists and eight to ten other part-time technicians. Expenditures were by then running at more than one million dollars a year.

Monsanto's overall research project was regarded as having five stages.

First came the development of fundamental scientific information on the bio-degradation of surfactants.[28] Next, a surfactant had to be designed to meet the following criteria: be highly biodegradable; be composed of raw materials available in large quantities; possess satisfactory functional and physical properties for a detergent; and be economically feasible. The third stage concerned the development of raw materials—their chemistry, the process of manufacturing, and the engineering and construction of the manufacturing facilities. After that the same aspects had to be considered in regard to development of the surfactants. Finally came the development of finished detergent products. This stage was one step beyond those in which the raw materials supplier was principally involved, but as factors here impinged on all the stages which preceded it, it could not be ignored. The last four stages had of necessity all to be conducted concurrently as they affected one another.

Monsanto and other suppliers advanced from production of small laboratory samples that had been tested and culled by their customers (Monsanto alone had submitted 123 such samples) to increasingly larger quantities. By June of 1963, they were producing tank-car lots of promising types of materials for larger scale tests run by producers of finished detergents. In early 1963, we recall, the industry had set a target date of December 31, 1965, for a complete changeover to the new detergents. The date was based on the declarations of suppliers and realistic estimates by producers of the time necessary to get the more degradable materials built into a finished product and it in turn into the hands of consumers. However, by June of 1963 Procter and Gamble was saying that it now expected to beat the target date by several months.[29]

On January 28, 1964, the Colgate-Palmolive Company made public the results of the first major field tests on the degradability of the new detergent formulations completed in the United States.[30] The results confirmed those of extensive laboratory and pilot plant tests and demonstrated the effectiveness under practical conditions of the new detergents that Colgate had produced and used in all of the tests and that it intended to sell on the market. Colgate was gratified to find that over 80 percent of the housewives using the new detergents in the field test considered them as good or better than any of the products they had previously used. Progress towards more biodegradable formulations was also being made by other detergent producers, and in July of 1964 the industry advanced its target date for complete conversion to the new detergents by six months to June 30, 1965.[31] The date is significant—it is that specified in the bills on detergents introduced in Congress early in 1963 principally by Representative Reuss and Senator Nelson. Voluntary action would achieve what law would have required.

Prior to the changeover, monitoring of some twenty sewage plants around the nation began in late 1964.[32] Surfactant concentrations were determined by the methylene blue active substance (MBAS) analysis. The switchover to LAS was to be considered a success if the MBAS level of a plant's effluent could be reduced to 1 mg/l or less. This concentration was chosen since ABS or LAS or a mixture of both could produce incipient foaming in streams at a level of about 1 mg/l or above.

Tests at the Columbus, Ohio, sewage treatment plant were started in October, 1964, just as the conversion to LAS was getting under way. At that time MBAS levels in the influent to the plant were as high as 9 mg/l. By June of 1965 they had dropped to 3–4 mg/l, and were to remain in this range throughout the period of testing. Effluent levels from the plant were about 3 mg/l in October, 1964; by the following June they had dropped to 1 mg/l, where they remained throughout the testing period. During this period, removal of ABS/LAS increased from 60 to 70 and then to almost 90 percent. Differential infrared analyses of the influent to the plant showed that only a small amount of branched-chain material was still present by the end of the study. Similar results were reported from the other plants monitored, including the Hyperion plant in Los Angeles, one of the largest and best-known sewage treatment plants in the nation and which was designed to treat most of the city's sewage. In general, most plants, and not only those monitored by the industry, reported a disappearance of the foaming problems previously encountered.

However, about a third of the homes in the United States were not linked with public sewage facilities, and here the detergent pollution problem persisted.[33] Suffolk County in Long Island, New York, continued to provide perhaps the best example of the problem. Households there, we recall, generally used cesspools to receive their waste products; and water for many of the households came from on-site wells. Tests conducted in Suffolk County showed that where wastes went directly into the water table, the removal of any soluble organic material, including LAS, was incomplete. The Soap and Detergent Association argued that the problem lay in the inadequacy of the cesspool systems rather than with LAS. Still, where a cesspool or septic tank system was operating under proper conditions, tests showed 87 percent degradation of LAS compared to 60.5 percent of ABS. There were some who thought that a third generation of detergents was called for, but the Soap and Detergent Association argued that the provision of sewers and public water supplies was the only way to avoid the problem.

Mounting a major effort, the American detergent industry had developed what would be an altogether satisfactory successor to ABS, namely, LAS. Sen. Gaylord Nelson noted how quickly the industry's April, 1963, statement of its intention to convert to a more biodegradable surfactant by the end of

1965 had followed upon the introduction of the House and Senate bills on detergents. He suggested that the bills were responsible for bringing about the conversion. But the industry, both in the United States and abroad, had been searching for several years prior to the introduction of the bills for a satisfactory substitute. And just about the time that political pressure was being exerted in the Congress, the problem was finally yielding to a technological solution.

The American industry had closely watched developments in Britain and initially had followed the British lead in obtaining straight-chain alkylate in the form of alpha-olefins from the cracking of wax. It also obtained such alkylate from the Ziegler polymerization of ethylene. But it was the utilization of the technology of molecular sieves to obtain normal-paraffins, coupled with the knowledge that alkylates in the C_{10} to C_{15} range were most readily biodegraded, that enabled progress to be made beyond the stages the British had reached in refining the wax-cracking process through the use of urea complexes. If government pressure had an effect anywhere in hastening the development of a new surfactant, it was in Britain. But that pressure had not yielded the use of molecular sieve technology there. From about 1958, following the completion of the first phase of its examination of the detergent pollution problem described earlier, the American industry knew that it, as the British and West German industries, would have to find a substitute for ABS. The subsequent passage of German legislation on detergents confirmed this view. Thus the American industry sought an alternative surfactant, and the culmination of its successful search roughly coincided with the introduction of Reuss's and Nelson's bills on detergents. If anything, the bills caused a more rapid conversion to the new surfactant, but they had no influence on its creation.

Epilogue

The Problem Solved: Biodegradable LAS

Although the U.S. Congress anticipated that the substitution of LAS for ABS would solve the detergent pollution problem, Sen. Gaylord Nelson continued to believe that in the public interest detergents should be regulated by law. However, his new bill introduced in early 1965 was overwhelmed by the rapidly accumulating evidence, reported to a watchful Congress, that the introduction of LAS had indeed solved the detergent pollution problem. West Germany and Britain soon reported similar results.

Some four months before the conversion to LAS was to be completed, Senator Nelson once again acted to have legislation passed concerning synthetic detergents. On March 10, 1965, he introduced S. 1479, a bill to amend the Federal Water Pollution Control Act by adding a new section twelve on detergents. In general this section was very similar to section twelve of S. 649, which had been deleted from that bill by the House Committee on Public Works in 1964. It would require the Secretary of HEW to appoint a technical committee to assist him or her in evaluating progress in the development of "decomposable" detergents and in setting standards of decomposability for such detergents. However, whereas in the earlier section twelve such standards were to be based on the latest scientific and technical knowledge available, now they were to be based on "tests which truly simulate" the operations of municipal sewage treatment plants and septic tanks, and up to $250,000 were to be provided to the secretary for making such tests.[1] Nelson was of course fully aware of the approaching conversion to LAS, but he wanted to have generated "the scientific data needed to evaluate it." He had had assurances from E. Scott Pattison, manager of the Soap and Detergent Association, that test procedures had been developed to assure that LAS was readily biodegradable; but Nelson's attitude was "that these tests are not carried out by any official Government agency and there is no way of being certain that they are adequate to protect the public interest."[2]

On May 21, 1965, Nelson explained the intent of his bill before a special subcommittee on air and water pollution of the Senate's Committee on Public Works, which was holding general hearings on progress and programs relating to the abatement of water pollution. James M. Quigley, assistant secretary of HEW, testified immediately after Nelson, and his remarks bore directly on Nelson's concerns. Quigley explained that when the detergent industry had declared its intention in June, 1963, of producing more readily biodegradable detergents, the Soap and Detergent Association had invited HEW to appoint an ex officio member to its biodegradation test method subcommittee.[3] Dr. Leon W. Weinberger, chief of the Department's Basic and Applied Sciences Branch, had been appointed to the subcommittee and he, or a member of his staff, had attended all of its subsequent meetings. In his capacity as a committee member, Weinberger had had access to all of the test data and research results from more than a dozen laboratories. He had been furnished with all data requested, and there had been no reluctance on the part of the industry to make its results available. The committee's goal was to develop a means of determining the biodegradability of LAS to compare with the biodegradability of ABS. Tentative standard test procedures for determining the relative biodegradabilities of LAS and ABS were now available.

Quigley reported that, based on the available laboratory evidence and field studies, LAS would be more readily biodegraded than ABS under aerobic conditions. His conclusion was based on the following: work carried out by his department's Division of Water Supply and Pollution Control; projects supported by the Soap and Detergent Association that were supervised by university researchers and whose data were available to departmental personnel; and projects supported by detergent formulators and supervised by university researchers, which were also "open" to departmental personnel. To Quigley there was clearly no question that LAS was more biodegradable than ABS. He found it significant that the degree of biodegradability of LAS was greater than that required under the West German law and that LAS appeared to be removed to a degree equal to or greater than the other organic materials found in sewage. In response to a question from Sen. Edmund Muskie, the Senate subcommittee's chairman, as to whether a satisfactory solution to the foaming problem had been achieved, Quigley added: "on the basis of evidence in so far, we have reason to be optimistic. But it is like testing an automobile in Detroit or testing a piece of field equipment in Aberdeen, until you get it out and actually drive it or fire it under wartime conditions you can't really ever be certain that it is as good as the Detroit car manufacturers say it is or the weapons technicians assure it is. The test must come in actual day-to-day practice."[4]

Industry representatives also testified; among them was the technical director of the Soap and Detergent Association, Charles G. Bueltman, who described controlled field studies that indicated "effective" biodegradability of LAS.[5] He discussed the results obtained at Woodbridge, Virginia (mentioned in chapter 5), and three additional test sites. At Brookside Estates, a residential development consisting of eighty-eight upper middle class homes just north of Columbus, Ohio, a twenty-month study conducted under a wide variety of operating conditions by Prof. G. P. Hanna of Ohio State University showed LAS removals of up to 93.5 percent. As in the Woodbridge Test, LAS removal was as good or better than that for normal sewage constituents, as determined by overall BOD removal. Under similar operating conditions average ABS removals had reached only 52.2 percent.

A third study, conducted under the supervision of Professors G. A. Rohlich and M. Starr Nichols of the University of Wisconsin, measured ABS/LAS removal in the extended aeration activated sludge plant of the Kettle Moraine Boys' School near Plymouth, Wisconsin. The results indicated a one-to-one ratio between LAS removal and BOD removal. The former ranged between 95 and 99 percent, as compared with the 75 to 85 percent ABS removal previously measured. Finally, Prof. John Knapp of Virginia Military Institute conducted a field test at Manassas Air Force Station, Virginia. Detention times in the station's activated sludge plant were typical of those common to large municipal sewage treatment plants. Once again, LAS removal very closely paralleled BOD removal. Also, results obtained when shorter detention times were employed clearly indicated a high degree of biodegradability for LAS.

Bueltman stressed that adequate sewage treatment facilities would be required if the full benefits of the industry's conversion program were to be realized. Yet 34 percent of the nation's houses were not connected to sewers, using instead septic tanks or, worse, cesspools. The Soap and Detergent Association had sponsored tests on septic tank-tile facilities under the supervision of Prof. P. H. McGauhey of the University of California.[6] McGauhey studied the removal not only of ABS and LAS but also of alcohol sulfate (AS), a surfactant that had been found to be highly degradable in a prototype septic tank-tile field system. Where it was possible to study removals under optimized conditions, LAS and AS were found to be removed 97 and 99 percent respectively, as compared with 74 percent for ABS. Thus again it appeared that LAS would be a distinct improvement over ABS if good individual household treatment were provided.

The Soap and Detergent Association, Bueltman continued, was cooperating in a study of the role of detergents in the pollution of groundwater by cesspool effluent on Long Island. Although in cesspools LAS proved to be slightly more degradable than ABS, these tests showed the impossibility of removing organic residues, including the best of biodegradable surfactants, by the use of cesspools. Observed Bueltman:

> Considering that cesspools are a "constructed" hole in the ground, and on Long Island frequently built down to, or very close to the surface of the ground water, it is not surprising that more than 2 years of study confirmed that nitrogen cycle compounds (indicators of undegraded sewage) and coliform bacteria (indicating the waste originated in a human intestinal tract) were found to be present at distances of 100 feet from the cesspool, a ground water pollution condition that is unrelated to the presence or absence of detergent residues. Obviously then, neither LAS nor AS, nor any other material, having the required cleaning properties of which we are aware, is going to relieve this type of gross ground water pollution.[7]

Senator Muskie was impressed with what the industry had been doing in regard to solving the detergent pollution problem. He wanted to "compliment the industry upon the sense of urgency which it has applied to this problem since the hearings two years ago. I think it is clear you have achieved meaningful results and that those results are in the public interest." He added, however, that "we still have the reservations which we must have until the product has been demonstrated, until we are sure that better results can't be achieved."[8] The Congress must have shared the optimistic wait-and-see outlook of Muskie and also of Quigley, since its attitude still seemed to be that such a bill as Nelson's was unnecessary.

In the spring of 1966, almost a year after the conversion from ABS to LAS had been completed, Muskie's subcommittee on air and water pollution held further hearings on bills to amend the Federal Water Pollution Control Act, including Nelson's S. 1479, which the detergent industry considered utterly unnecessary.[9] Indeed, Nelson himself publicly admitted that "the foaming problem has now all but disappeared."[10] Nevertheless, he was concerned that there was "some evidence" that LAS was not highly degraded under certain conditions occurring in household septic tanks and municipal sewage treatment plants; that it had "been reported" that the amounts of LAS now typically found in municipal sewage tended to reduce the efficiency of treatment plants by killing the bacteria that carried out sludge digestion; and that some studies had shown that undegraded "LAS detergents" in small concentrations were two to four times as toxic to some species of fish as ABS detergents.

In testifying for the detergent industry before the subcommittee on May 12, Charles Bueltman addressed these points. He stated again the Soap and Detergent Association's conviction that septic tank systems were not the most desirable means of sewage treatment and that in most areas they should be replaced as soon as possible by more advanced treatment facilities. But he added that in properly designed and operated septic tank systems, the detergent industry's products would be removed as readily as other household wastes. In municipal sewage plants, whether activated sludge treatment or trickling filter plants, Bueltman denied that there was any inhibition of bacteria by LAS.[11]

Regarding toxicity, Bueltman acknowledged that in laboratory tests LAS had in comparison to ABS "exhibited slightly higher fish toxicity levels," but he explained why the industry felt that any concern was unwarranted.[12] First, LAS was biodegraded much more quickly than ABS even where treatment was not available. Second, the levels of detergent residues actually found in surface waters were considerably below the levels at which problems were indicated in laboratory tests. Thirdly, the components of LAS to which fish were most sensitive were those destroyed first in biodegradation, so that any LAS fractions found in rivers would be less toxic, weight for weight, than the original material.

The Soap and Detergent Association had been careful to have a comparison made of the toxicities of ABS and LAS. Bernard L. Oser and Kenneth Morgareidge of the Food and Drug Research Laboratories, of Maspeth, New York, were contracted to do the study. Using rats they determined the acute oral toxicities, and the effects of subacute dietary intake, of both ABS and LAS. When samples were administered in water dispersion, the acute oral toxicity (i.e., that dose which is lethal to fifty percent of the test animals) was found to be 0.52 g/kg for ABS and 0.65 g/kg for LAS, the difference between these values being considered as "not statistically significant."[13] Oser and Morgareidge then fed weanling rats ABS or LAS mixed with their diets in dosages of 0.05 and 0.25 g/kg/day for twelve weeks. When the animals had reached maturity, these dosages were provided by dietary concentrations of 1,000 and 5,000 ppm, respectively. (The 1962 USPHS drinking water standards had permitted a concentration of ABS of up to 0.5 ppm.) The rats developed normally and showed no changes related to ingestion of the test material in any of the several parameters examined, with the possible exception of a slight increase in liver weight. This effect was seen in both sexes at the higher dosage of ABS, but only in the females of the group fed 5,000 ppm LAS. No accompanying morphologic changes were seen in these livers on microscopic examination.

Bueltman went on to testify that conversion to LAS had been completed at production plants by June of 1965 as planned, and furthermore that the high expectations held for the biodegradability of LAS based on laboratory and controlled field testing had been borne out in nine months of actual experience in sewage treatment plants throughout the country. Five sites had been selected on the basis of their size and location and also to typify the conditions found nationally in secondary sewage treatment plants: Columbus, Ohio; Milwaukee, Wisconsin; Los Angeles and Livermore, California; and San Antonio, Texas. Scientists and engineers from government, industry, and universities, as well as sewage treatment plant operators, measured the surfactant contents of the raw wastes entering, and of the treated wastes leaving, the plants. They used the methylene blue standard analytical test to determine how much ABS and/or LAS was in the wastewaters, and reported the results in terms of methylene blue active substances (MBAS). In all cases three significant findings were obtained. The MBAS going into the plants were reduced, suggesting that degradation was occurring in the sewers leading to the plants; the MBAS within the plants were reduced, showing high biodegradation under the treatment process; and the MBAS leaving the plants were reduced, meaning that the amounts of MBAS entering receiving waters was much lower than before. The apparent breakdown of LAS on its way to a plant was an unexpected, but welcome, finding that had also been noted in Britain and West Germany.[14] Bueltman considered all three findings as "positive evidence of the impact of our industry's conversion from ABS to LAS." The president of the Soap and Detergent Association, Walter A. Hahn, asserted that "we have successfully lived up to the confidence you placed in our industry when you gave us the opportunity to put the voluntary approach into practice."[15]

The industry continued its monitoring program, and some twenty months after the conversion to LAS, *Chemical and Engineering News* published a brief article on the program's results under the title "LAS Detergents and Problems of Stream Foam." It stated that the data showed that LAS degraded more, and at a faster rate, than ABS and that "talk of a third-generation household detergent material that could replace LAS on the score of biodegradability is merely talk." At all plants monitored, effluent MBAS levels had dropped down to or below 1 mg/l, the concentration at which incipient foaming might occur. However, the results of tests carried out in Suffolk County, Long Island, by the temporary New York State Water Resources Planning Commission showed that where wastes went directly into the water table, the removal of any soluble organic material, including LAS, was incomplete. *Chemical and Engineering News* noted the industry's view that the problem lay in "the inadequacies of cesspool systems rather than in the LAS itself."[16]

It will be recalled that the West German government had legislated that from October 1, 1964, anionic detergents sold in the federal republic had to be at least 80 percent degradable. In 1967 the chairman of the country's Committee on Detergents and Water, Professor W. Husmann, reported that the efforts made to solve the detergent pollution problem had been successful. The degradability of anionic detergents now being marketed in Germany ranged from 85 to 95 percent. The overall degradation of detergents between the time of leaving households and that of emerging from sewage treatment plants exceeded 80 percent. Also, the decrease in the detergent content of rivers between 1964, before the detergent law went into force, and 1965 ranged from a minimum of 33 percent to a maximum of 77 percent. Said Husmann: "The mountains of foam on the water have mostly vanished. Here and there they may still appear, due to purely local conditions, but the times when whole sections of a river were covered with high mountains of foam are over." [17] He emphasized, however, and the American Soap and Detergent Association would have agreed that the "final solution" of the detergent pollution problem would be realized only when sufficient biological sewage treatment plants were built and were functioning efficiently.

Meanwhile in Britain, more of the new, improved surfactant, Dobane JNX sulfonate, had become available following the Luton experiment. Its use was extended, and eventually the manufacturers were able to give an understanding through the Confederation of British Industry that after December 31, 1964—six months before the completion of the American detergent industry's conversion to LAS—they would cease to incorporate any of the old surfactant in detergents. By 1967 the proportion of residual surfactant present in normal sewage effluent had fallen to about one-third of that present when the old surfactant, Dobane PT sulfonate, had been used. Whereas at most sewage works the residue from the old material had been about 35 percent at best, at a works producing a normal 30:20 effluent the residue from the new material varied between 10 and 15 percent. [18] Where an effluent of better quality was discharged, the residue was rarely more than 10 percent, and instances of average removals of 95 percent had been noted. In terms of concentration, few effluents of satisfactory standard contained more than 2 mg/l of surfactant. The highest quality effluents might carry less than 1 mg/l and be reluctant to produce foam even before, let alone after, dilution with river water. Sewage works had also reported a reduction in the intensity of foaming on activated-sludge plants and a consequent savings in anti-foam agents.

By 1967 it had not yet been possible to assess reliably the effect of the changeover to the new surfactants upon British rivers. There appeared to be an appreciable time lag between the general reduction of the surfactant concentration in effluents and an improvement in rivers. However, in some rivers, particularly the Thames and Lea for which very full records were available, there had been a striking reduction in the concentration of surfactant. Furthermore, river authorities in most parts of the country had observed a reduction in the foaming of their rivers. Thus in Britain by 1967 "the problem of synthetic detergents which loomed so large in the early fifties [was] now in sight of a solution." [19] As in the United States and West Germany, the change had come through the replacement of ABS by LAS. The latter had all the excellent properties of the former, and in addition was highly degradable.

In this study two transformations in the detergent industry, a major one and a minor one, have been described. The former saw the extensive substitution in the United States, Great Britain, and West Germany of soap by synthetic detergents from the late 1940s, the latter the replacement of the partially degradable ABS, the most popular surfactant incorporated in synthetic detergents prior to 1965, by the highly degradable LAS in mid-1965. The latter was dictated by public and government pressure, the former not. The emphasis has been on the latter transformation, and the perspective that of the social choice of technology.

In the preface I outlined four types of opposition that may be exerted against controversial technologies, two of which were seen in this study, namely, in-house opposition and what is generally the first type of public opposition to be expressed—that involving government. No one saw the need to proceed beyond the latter to the other public types, that is, either to take the detergent industry to court to force ABS off the market, or, having failed in court, to take direct physical action, such as sabotage, against the industry. The harm associated with the detergent pollution problem never became so threatening as to evoke such actions. Moreover, the industry found a solution satisfactory to all.

At the in-house level of opposition, involving sewage treatment and water purification plant operators, academic sanitary engineers, industrial and governmental technical personnel, and professional organizations, the problem of foaming caused by detergents was quickly noted. It was soon analyzed by Prof. Clair N. Sawyer and his colleagues in sanitary engineering at MIT. Although for some time the industry denied any causal connection between detergents and foaming, it meanwhile became active in investigating the problem, initially with the hope of saving the excellent and profitable ABS. The industry examined every aspect of the problem, certainly in its own self-interest but not without a sense of social responsibility. Had a satisfactory technological solution been at hand when the detergent pollution problem first erupted, it likely would have been implemented by the industry; but a decade's intensive research was required before such a solution was reached.

In the meantime the problem was taken up at the public level of opposition, where among other things government becomes involved. At this level the American experience differed from the British and German experiences. The British got to work on the problem almost as soon as it arose, creating committees that reported to the Minister of Housing and Local Government. The committees requested and received the cooperation of industry in investigating the problem, and they were able to call upon various governmental technical groups for advice and assistance in testing. In Britain the government's attitude was that it was responsible for seeing that the problem was solved, and that industry should cooperate with it in achieving a solution.

British tradition has long been to favor limits on government power when seeking solutions to problems caused by industrialization. The British Standing Technical Committee on Synthetic Detergents rejected the idea of restrictive legislation concerning synthetic detergents because the British detergent industry was making satisfactory progress toward a soft surfactant and because the committee believed that legislation would only retard further progress.

In West Germany, in contrast, the Bundestag legislated that by October 1, 1964, anionic surfactants in laundry and cleaning compounds sold on the market must be at least 80 percent degradable. In the United States the problem was monitored by HEW, which unlike the British Ministry of Housing and Local Government did not create a special committee for its study, being content to watch the situation through established agencies, especially the Taft Center for Sanitary Engineering in Cincinnati, Ohio. Eventually a few members of the U.S. Congress, principally Rep. Henry Reuss and Sen. Gaylord Nelson, both Democrats from Wisconsin, attempted to have the United States follow the German lead; but their attempt to ban the manufacture and importation of hard detergents through amendments to the Water Pollution Control Act proved unsuccessful. Given a tradition in the United States similar to the British one in the area of public policy, and given the greater progress that was being made by the American detergent industry toward a soft surfactant during 1963 and 1964, when bills that would regulate the nature of detergents were before the Congress, it was not surprising that a willing industry was allowed, as it had requested, to implement its promised solution voluntarily. It did so successfully. Like Britain, and in contrast to West Germany, the United States avoided the drawbacks that legislation would have entailed and that had been pointed out in 1963 by the American Water Works Association. The principal drawback was the waste of money and the misuse of scientific talent that the testing of numerous products would have caused.

Nevertheless, the American detergent industry had worked under the threat of legislative action. With the passage of the Water Pollution Control Act and the successive amendments to it, Congress had made clear from 1948 its intention in regard to water pollution. In addition, in the United States the late 1950s witnessed the incipient environmental movement to which, as I have argued in the introduction, concern about water pollution was central from its beginning. But at best the threat merely shortened the time, by how much is impossible to say, that elapsed between the development of the molecular sieve, normal-paraffin route to LAS in 1962–63 and the complete conversion from ABS to LAS by the end of June, 1965. The development of the molecular sieve route was in its early stages before Reuss introduced the first detergent bill in early 1963.

The different governmental approaches in dealing with the detergent industries to solve the pollution problem in the three countries—the formal British cooperative and the informal, voluntary American cooperative on the one hand, and the West German legislative on the other—all led to the same satisfactory outcome. In LAS, American, British, and West German societies had been provided with a product, a technology, that all found acceptable.

Appendix I

West German Act Concerning Detergents in Washing and Cleansing Media of 5 September 1961

Article 1

(1) It is the purpose of this Act to achieve maximum decomposability of surface-active and cleansing agents (detergents) contained in washing and cleansing media.

(2) Washing and cleansing media containing detergents shall not be put on the market by the manufacturer or importer, unless the decomposability of the detergents meets the requirements of the statutory ordinance to be issued under article 2.

(3) Paragraph 2 shall not apply where washing and cleansing media are supplied to third persons as samples for testing and experimental purposes.

(4) Nor shall paragraph 2 apply to the export or transit of washing and cleansing media.

(5) Any other conveyance of washing and cleansing media into or out of the area to which this Act applies shall be deemed to be import or export.

Article 2

(1) The Federal Government shall be authorized to establish, by a statutory ordinance requiring the consent of the Bundesrat, the requirements of decomposability with regard to detergents in washing and cleansing media, as well as the necessary methods of testing. Such requirements must be in keeping with the level of scientific knowledge and technology attained in the field of detergent manufacture and sewage plant efficiency.

(2) The Federal Government shall issue the first statutory ordinance under paragraph 1 not later than 30 June 1962.

Article 3

(1) The authority competent under land legislation may take samples of washing and cleansing media needed for inspection at the importers' or manufacturers' prem-

ises. Part of the sample, officially packed and sealed, shall be left behind, if so demanded.

(2) The persons commissioned by the competent authority shall be permitted to enter rooms and premises in so far as their duty so requires. The fundamental right of inviolability of the home as defined by Article 13 of the Basic Law shall be restricted to that extent.

(3) The officials of the authority competent under Land legislation or their authorized agents shall not, without authority, disclose or make use of any business or technical secrets which have become known to them in the course of their duties, even if they are no longer in the service or if their employment has come to an end. This shall also apply to other persons who, by reason of official reporting, have obtained knowledge of the facts stated in the first sentence.

Article 4

(1) Any person violating the obligation imposed on him by virtue of paragraph 3 of article 3 shall be liable to imprisonment for a term not exceeding one year and a fine, or to either of these penalties.

(2) If the offender acts for remuneration or with the intent to secure pecuniary benefit for himself or for a third person, or to cause damage to a third person, he shall be liable to imprisonment for a term not exceeding two years. In addition, a fine may be imposed.

(3) Prosecution shall only take place upon petition of the injured person.

Article 5

(1) Any person who, in his capacity as a manufacturer or importer, deliberately puts washing or cleansing media on the market which do not meet the provisions of article 1, shall be guilty of a statutory offense.

(2) A statutory offense may render the offender liable to
a. a fine not exceeding DM 10,000, where such offense has been committed intentionally;
b. a fine not exceeding DM 5,000, where such offense has been committed negligently.

Article 6

(1) The provision in respect of fines contained in article 5 shall also apply to any person acting as an executive organ on behalf of, and authorized to represent, a body corporate, or as a member of any such organ, or as the legal representative of a third person. This shall also apply if the legal act establishing the representatives authority is void.

(2) Any person charged with the management or supervision of the enterprise or

of part of the enterprise of a third person, or who is expressly entrusted by such third person to fulfill, on his own responsibility, any duties imposed by this Act shall be accorded the same legal treatment as persons specified in paragraph 1.

Article 7

(1) If, in an enterprise, any person commits an act subject to a fine under paragraph 1 of article 5, the owner or manager of the enterprise or the owner's legal representative or a member of the executive organ in charge of the legal representation of a body corporate or a partner authorized to represent a partnership (Personengesellschaft) under German commercial law may be liable to a fine, provided that they have failed in their duty of supervision either intentionally or negligently and the offense is attributable thereto. The amount of the fine shall be determined in accordance with paragraph 2 of article 5.

Article 8

(1) If any person, in his capacity as a member of the executive organ in charge of the legal representation or as a "Prokurist" of a body corporate or as a partner authorized to represent a partnership under German commercial law or as a "Prokurist" of a partnership, commits a statutory offense under the provisions of paragraph 1 of article 5, a fine to be determined in accordance with paragraph 2 of article 5 may also be imposed on the body corporate or the partnership.

(2) Article 6 of the Law on Statutory Offenses shall also apply in respect of any remuneration or profit which the body corporate or the partnership under German commercial law has received in consideration of the statutory offense or derived therefrom.

Article 9

Objects may be confiscated which are connected with an offense punishable under paragraph 1 of article 5. Paragraph 4 of article 18 and articles 19 to 26 of the Law on Statutory Offences shall apply correspondingly.

Article 10

In accordance with paragraph 1 of article 13 of the Third Transition Act of 4 January 1952 (BGBl I, p. 1), this Act shall also be valid in the Land Berlin. Statutory ordinances made under this Act shall apply to the Land Berlin in accordance with article 14 of the Third Transition Act.

Article 11

This Act shall come into force on the day following its promulgation. The constitutional rights of the Bundesrat have been observed. The foregoing Act is hereby promulgated.

Bonn, 5 September 1961.

(Federal Republic of Germany, Ministry of Health, "Development of the Detergent Problem in the Federal Republic of Germany," in U.S. Congress, Senate, *Water Pollution Control*, Hearings Before a Special Subcommittee on Air and Water Pollution on the Committee on Public Works, 88th Cong., 1st sess. (June 17, 18, 19, 20, 25 and 26, 1963), pp. 352–54.)

Appendix II

H.R. 4571, 88th Cong., 1st sess.

A Bill to amend the Federal Water Pollution Control Act to protect the navigable waters of the United States from further pollution by requiring that synthetic petroleum-based detergents manufactured in the United States or imported into the United States comply with certain standards of decomposability

Be it enacted by the Senate and House of Representatives of the United States of America in Congress assembled, That the Federal Water Pollution Control Act (33 U.S.C. 466–466k) is amended by redesignating sections 10 through 14 as sections 11 through 15, respectively, and by inserting immediately after section 9 thereof the following new section:

Regulation Of Detergents

"Sec. 10 (a) The Congress finds that the navigable waters of the United States are being irreparably polluted through the ever-increasing discharge into such waters of synthetic petroleum-based detergents which decompose slowly or do not decompose at all. The Congress further finds that to prevent the further pollution of the navigable waters of the United States in the public interest it must regulate the composition of detergents which will eventually be discharged into the navigable waters of the United States, but because of the impossibility of determining and thereby effectively regulating only those detergents it must regulate all detergents manufactured in the United States or imported into the United States. Therefore, it is the policy of the Congress by the enactment of this section to invoke and exercise its fullest constitutional powers in order to effectively regulate the composition of all such detergents.

"(b) It shall be unlawful for any person to import into the United States or manufacture in the United States any detergent after June 30, 1965, unless such detergent conforms with standards of decomposability prescribed pursuant to subsection (c) of this section.

"(c) The Secretary shall, on or before the one hundred and eightieth day after the date of enactment of this section prescribe and publish in the Federal Register standards of decomposability for detergents, based on the latest scientific and technical knowledge available with respect to the manufacture of detergents and the operation of sewage treatment systems, which will assure that all detergents manufactured in the United States or imported into the United States after June 30, 1965, will decompose reasonably quickly and completely after use. Included with such standards shall be specific methods by which detergents shall be tested by the Secretary to determine if they conform to such standards. Such standards shall be the sole standards of decomposability applicable to any detergent manufactured in or imported into the United States.

"(d) (1) Any detergent which does not conform with standards prescribed pursuant to subsection (c) of this section shall be liable to be proceeded against on libel of information and condemned in any district court in the United States within the jurisdiction of which such detergent is found.

"(2) Such detergent shall be liable to seizure by process pursuant to the libel, and the procedure in cases under this subsection shall conform, as nearly as may be, to the procedure in admiralty; except that on demand of either party any issue of fact joined in any such case shall be tried by jury. When libel for condemnation proceedings under this subsection, involving the same claimant and the same issues, are pending in two or more jurisdictions, such pending proceedings, upon application of the United States or the claimant seasonably made to the court of one such jurisdiction, shall be consolidated for trial by order of such court, and tried in (A) any district selected by the applicant where one of such proceedings is pending; or (B) a district agreed upon by stipulation between the parties. If no order for consolidation is so made within a reasonable time, the United States or the claimant may apply to the court of one such jurisdiction, and such court (after giving the other party, the claimant, or the United States attorney for such district, reasonable notice and opportunity to be heard) shall by order, unless good cause to the contrary is shown, specify a district of reasonable proximity to the claimant's principal place of business, in which all such pending proceedings shall be consolidated for trial and tried. Such order of consolidation shall not apply so as to require the removal of any case the date for trial of which has been fixed. The court granting such order shall give prompt notification thereof to the other courts having jurisdiction of the cases covered thereby.

"(3) Any detergent condemned under this subsection shall, after entry of the decree, be disposed of by the destruction or sale as the court may, in accordance with the provisions of this subsection, direct and the proceeds thereof, if sold, less the legal costs and charges, shall be paid into the Treasury of the United States; but such detergent shall not be sold under such decree for a use which would result in the pollution of the navigable waters of the United States contrary to subsection (a) of this section; except that after entry of the decree and upon the payment of the costs of such proceedings and the execution of a good and sufficient bond conditioned that such detergent shall not be sold or disposed of contrary to the provisions of this section, the court may by order direct that such detergent be delivered to the owner thereof to be destroyed or brought into compliance with the provisions of this section under the supervision of an officer or employee duly designated by the Secretary, and the expenses of such supervision shall be paid by the person obtaining release of the detergent under bond.

"(4) When a decree of condemnation is entered against the detergent, court costs and fees, and storage and other proper expenses, shall be awarded against the person, if any, intervening as claimant of the detergent.

"(5) In the case of removal for trial of any case as provided by paragraph (2) of this subsection—

"(A) the clerk of the court from which removal is made shall promptly transmit to the court in which the case is to be tried all records in the case necessary in order that such court may exercise jurisdiction;

"(B) the court to which such case is removed shall have the powers and be subject to the duties, for purposes of such case, which the court from which removal was made would have had, or to which such court would have been subject, if such case had not been removed.

"(e) (1) The United States district courts shall have jurisdiction, for cause shown and subject to the provisions of rule 65 (a) and (b) of the Federal Rules of Civil Procedure, to restrain violations of this section.

"(2) In any proceeding for criminal contempt for violation of an injunction on restraining order issued under this subsection, which violation also constitutes a violation of this section, trial shall be by the court or, upon demand of the accused, by a jury. Such trial shall be conducted in accordance with the practice and procedure applicable in the case of proceedings subject to the provisions of rule 42(b) of the Federal Rules of Criminal Procedure.

"(f) All libel or injunction proceedings for the enforcement, or to restrain violations, of this section shall be by and in the name of the United States. Subpoenas for witnesses who are required to attend a court of the United States in any district may run into any other district in any such proceeding.

"(g) The Secretary of the Treasury and the Secretary shall jointly prescribe regulations for the efficient enforcement of the provisions of subsection (i) of this section, except as otherwise provided therein. Such regulations shall be promulgated in such manner and take effect at such time, after due notice, as the Secretary shall determine.

"(h) (1) The Secretary is authorized to conduct examinations, inspections, and investigations for the purposes of this section through officers and employees of the Department of Health, Education, and Welfare or through any health officer or employee of any State, or political subdivision thereof, duly commissioned by the Secretary.

"(2) For purposes of enforcement of this section, officers or employees duly designated by the Secretary, upon presenting appropriate credentials and a written notice to the owner, operator, or agent in charge, are authorized (A) to enter, at reasonable times, any factory, warehouse, or establishment in which detergents are manufactured, processed, packed, or held, or to enter any vehicle being used to transport or hold such detergents; (B) to inspect, at reasonable times and within reasonable limits and in a reasonable manner, such factory warehouse, establishment, or vehicle, and all pertinent equipment, finished and unfinished materials; and (C) to obtain samples of such materials. A separate notice shall be given for each such inspection, but a notice shall not be required for each entry made during the period covered by the inspection. Each such inspection shall be commenced and completed with reasonable promptness.

"(3) If the officer or employee obtains any sample, prior to leaving the premises, he shall give to the owner, operator, or agent in charge a receipt describing the samples obtained. If an analysis is made of such sample, a copy of the results of such analysis shall be furnished promptly to the owner, operator, or agent in charge.

"(i) (1) The Secretary of the Treasury shall deliver to the Secretary, upon his request, samples of detergents which are being imported or offered for import into the United States, giving notice thereof to the owner or consignee, who may appear before the Surgeon General and have the right to introduce testimony. If it appears from the examination of such samples or otherwise that such detergent does not conform to standards prescribed pursuant to subsection (c) of this section, such detergent shall be refused admission, except as provided in paragraph (2) of this subsection. The Secretary of the Treasury shall cause the destruction of any such detergent refused admission unless such detergent is exported, under regulations prescribed by the Secretary of the Treasury, within ninety days of the date of notice of such refusal or within such additional time as may be permitted pursuant to such regulations.

"(2) Pending decision as to the admission of a detergent being imported or offered for import, the Secretary of the Treasury may authorize delivery of such detergent to the owner or consignee upon the execution by him of a good and sufficient bond providing for the payment of such liquidated damages in the event of default as may be required pursuant to regulations of the Secretary of the Treasury.

"(j) As used in this section, the term 'detergent' means any synthetic foaming surface active cleaning agent."

(U.S. Congress, House, Water Pollution Control Act Amendments, Hearings before the Committee on Public Works, 88th Cong., 1st sess. (December 4, 5, 6, 9 and 10, 1963), 2d sess. (February 4, 5, 6, 7, 18 and 19, 1964), pp. 7–9.)

Notes

Introduction

1. Samuel P. Hays, *Beauty, Health, and Permanence: Environmental Politics in the United States, 1955–1985*, p. 2; "From Conservation to Environment: Environmental Politics in the United States Since World War Two," *Environmental Review*, 6, no. 2 (Fall, 1982): 14.

2. Hays, *Beauty, Health, and Permanence*, p. 13.

3. Ibid., pp. 52, 54, 55–56.

4. J. Clarence Davies III and Barbara S. Davies, *The Politics of Pollution*, 2d ed., pp. 7–10.

5. Barry Commoner, *The Closing Circle: Nature, Man, and Technology*.

6. Davies and Davies, *The Politics of Pollution*, p. 8.

7. Hays, "From Conservation to Environment," p. 20.

8. Ibid., p. 21.

9. Ibid., p. 24.

10. Davies and Davies, *The Politics of Pollution*, p. 9.

11. Ibid., pp. 28–29.

12. Leonard B. Dworsky, *Pollution*, vol. 1 of *Conservation in the United States: A Documentary History*, ed. Frank E. Smith, pp. 26–27.

13. Davies and Davies, *The Politics of Pollution*, p. 31.

14. Dworsky, *Pollution*, p. 29.

15. Ibid., p. 30.

16. In addition to his work cited in the succeeding footnotes, see the following: Joel A. Tarr, "The Separate vs. Combined Sewer Problem: A Case Study in Urban Technology Design Choice," *Journal of Urban History*, 5, no. 3 (May, 1979): 308–39; Joel A. Tarr, with James McCurley III, Francis C. McMichael, and Terry Yosie, "Water and Wastes: A Retrospective Assessment of Wastewater Technology in the United States, 1800–1932," *Technology and Culture*, 25, no. 2 (Apr., 1984): 226–63; and Joel A. Tarr, "Industrial Wastes and Public Health: Some Historical Notes, Part I, 1876–1932," *American Journal of Public Health*, 75, no. 9 (Sept., 1985): 1059–67.

17. Joel A. Tarr and Francis Clay McMichael, "Decisions about Wastewater Technology: 1850–1932," *Journal of the Water Resources Planning and Management Division, Proceedings of the American Society of Civil Engineers*, 103, no. WR1 (May, 1977): p. 49, 50.

18. Ibid., p. 53.

19. Joel A. Tarr, Terry Yosie, and James McCurley III, "Disputes over Water Quality Policy: Professional Cultures in Conflict, 1900–1917," *American Journal of Public Health*, 70, no. 4 (Apr., 1980): 432.

20. Joel A. Tarr, "The Search for the Ultimate Sink: Urban Air, Land, and Water Pollution in Historical Perspective," *Records of the Columbia Historical Society of Washington, D.C.*, 51 (1984): 8.

21. Joel A. Tarr, Francis C. McMichael, et al., "Retrospective Assessment of Waste Water Technology in the United States: 1800–1972," (A Report to the National Science Foundation/RANN, Carnegie-Mellon University, October, 1977, Typescript), pp. vii–19.

22. Ibid., p. vii–37.

23. William McGucken, *Scientists, Society, and State: The Social Relations of Science Movement in Great Britain, 1931–1947*, pp. 129–30.

24. Edward W. Lawless suspects a connection here with the growth of the chemical and pharmaceutical industries. See his *Technology and Social Shock*, pp. 486–87.

25. Allan Mazur, *The Dynamics of Technical Controversy*.

26. See, for example, Thomas R. Dunlap, *DDT: Scientists, Citizens, and Public Policy.*

27. See, for example, Dorothy Nelkin and Michael Pollak, *The Atom Besieged: Extraparliamentary Dissent in France and Germany.*

28. Barry Commoner, "A Reporter at Large: The Environment," *New Yorker*, 63, no. 17, June 15, 1987, p. 57.

29. Ibid., p. 64.

30. Hays, *Beauty, Health, and Permanence*, p. 52.

31. Dworsky, *Pollution*, pp. 23–26.

Chapter I. The Coming of Synthetic Detergents

1. F. W. Gibbs, "The History of the Manufacture of Soap," *Annals of Science*, 4 (1939): 169–190; Charles Singer et al., eds., *A History of Technology*, 1:260, 261; 2:355–56; 3:169–71, 175, 703–705; 4:61, 232, 235, 238, 241, 246, 253–54; 5:317, 828, 834.

2. All fatty oils and fats are mixtures of glycerides, which are esters of the trihydric alcohol glycerol and some fatty acid such as palmitic acid. The chemistry involved in soap manufacture may be illustrated as follows:

$$C_3H_5(OCOC_{15}H_{31})_3 + 3NaOH \rightarrow 3NaOCOC_{15}H_{31} + C_3H_5(OH)_3$$

palmitin   + caustic soda → sodium palmitate + glycerol
(fat)   (soap)

The reaction of fat with caustic soda is called saponification.

3. H. C. E. Johnson, "Is Soap Slipping?" *Scientific American* 175, no. 1, Aug., 1946, p. 58.

4. Laurence M. Kushner and James I. Hoffman, "Synthetic Detergents," *Scientific American* 185, no. 4, Oct., 1951, p. 26.

5. T. E. Larson, "Synthetic Detergents," *Journal/American Water Works Association* 41, no. 4 (Apr., 1949): 315.

6. R. Norris Shreve, *Chemical Process Industries*, 3d ed., p. 546.

7. Donald Price, *Detergents: What They Are and What They Do*, p. 36.

8. Benjamin Levitt, *Oils, Detergents and Maintenance Specialities*, 1:54, 55.

9. J. L. Molliet, B. Collie, and W. Black, *Surface Activity: The Physical Chemistry, Technical Applications, and Chemical Constitution of Synthetic Surface-active Agents*, 2d ed., p. 355.

10. Price, *Detergents*, pp. 37–38; A. Davidsohn and B. M. Milwidsky, *Synthetic Detergents*, 5th ed., p. 2; Molliet, Collie, and Black, *Surface Activity*, pp. 356–57.

11. Price, *Detergents*, p. 38.

12. Merritt L. Kastens and Jackson J. Ayo, Jr., "Pioneer Surfactant," *Industrial and Engineering Chemistry* 42, no. 9 (Sept., 1950): 1626.

13. Price, *Detergents*, p. 41.

14. Kastens and Ayo, "Pioneer Surfactant," p. 1626; Kushner and Hoffman, "Synthetic Detergents," p. 26. A molecule of sodium laurate, a typical soap, consists of a long chain of hydrogen and carbon atoms ending in a group of carbon, oxygen, and sodium atoms; the first part is a hydrocarbon, and the second is a sodium carboxylate group:

Sodium laurate

One of the earliest synthetic detergents, sodium dodecyl sulfate, has a molecule that is strikingly similar:

Sodium dodecyl sulfate

It differs from the sodium laurate molecule principally in the replacement of the sodium carboxylate group by the sulfate ester group. Sodium dodecyl sulfate has a cleaning ability comparable to that of soap, yet its chemical nature is such that, unlike soap, it does not react with hard water or acids (Kushner and Hoffman).

15. Kastens and Ayo, "Pioneer Surfactant," p. 1626.

16. Ibid.

17. Ibid., pp. 1626, 1627.

18. G. F. Longman, *The Analysis of Detergents and Detergent Products*, p. 14.

19. Charles Wilson, *The History of Unilever: A Study in Economic Growth and Social Change*, 2:351.

20. "'Dreft' Led the Way," *Soap and Chemical Specialties* 34, no. 9 (Sept., 1958): 48, 47.

21. Ibid., p. 49; Wilson, *History of Unilever*, 2:351.

22. F. H. Braybrook, "The Development of Synthetic Detergents and Future Trends," *Chemistry and Industry* (June 26, 1948): 405.

23. Wilson, *History of Unilever*, 3:229.

24. "'Dreft' Led the Way," p. 47.

25. Oscar Schisgall, *Eyes on Tomorrow: The Evolution of Procter and Gamble,* p. 172.

26. Ibid.; "'Dreft' Led the Way," pp. 49–50.

27. Wilson, *History of Unilever,* 3:229.

28. *New York Times,* Oct. 15, 1948, p. 19.

29. A. B. Hersberger and C. P. Neidig, "Present Status of Organic Synthetic Detergents," *Chemical and Engineering News* 27, no. 23 (June 6, 1949): 1648.

30. Braybrook, "The Development of Synthetic Detergents," p. 404.

31. A. K. Simcox, "The Future of Synthetic Detergents in Relation to the Petroleum-Chemical Industry," *Chemistry and Industry* (Mar. 11, 1950): 178.

32. The word "alkylation" derives from the word "alkyl," meaning a univalent aliphatic radical of the form C_nH_{2n+1}. To alkylate a compound means to introduce one or more alkyl groups into it.

33. Toluene, an aromatic hydrocarbon (C_7H_8) that resembles benzene, is another petroleum product, the production of which was also developed on a large scale during the war by special processes devised within the petroleum industry. During the war toluene was used both in aviation fuel and in the manufacture of explosives. Braybrook, "The Development of Synthetic Detergents," p. 405.

34. Propylene tetramer, a polymer formed from four molecules of the monomer propylene (C_3H_6), was produced using polymerization methods also developed in the petroleum industry; Longman, *The Analysis of Detergents and Detergent Products,* p. 17.

35. Hersberger and Neidig, "Present Status of Organic Synthetic Detergents," p. 1648; Davidsohn and Milwidsky, *Synthetic Detergents,* p. 3. Tetrapropylene is chemically identical to propylene tetramer, but it is derived from a kerosene fraction instead of being polymerized from propylene. A key step in the formulation of alkyl benzene sulfonate was the alkylation of benzene. This involved the chlorination of a kerosene fraction and subsequent union with benzene through the Friedel-Crafts reaction, in which a monochlorinated product is reacted with benzene in the presence of aluminum chloride as catalyst.

$$C_{12}H_{26} \; + \; Cl_2 \longrightarrow C_{12}H_{25}Cl \; + \; HCl$$

$$C_{12}H_{25}Cl \; + \; \bigcirc \longrightarrow C_{12}H_{25}\!\!-\!\!\bigcirc \; + \; HCl$$

In the United States the product commonly used in the chlorination operation was the saturated kerosene fraction from a Pennsylvania- or Michigan-type crude oil. In the alkylation stage benzene and anhydrous aluminum chloride were placed together in a reacting vessel and the chlorinated hydrocarbon was slowly added. When the reaction was complete, the alkyl benzene compound was separated by fractionation. The final step was that of sulfonation. John W. McCutcheon, *Synthetic Detergents,* pp. 188–94.

36. O. M. Morgan and Leslie C. Wizemann, "Growth of the Anionics," *Soap and Chemical Specialties* 34, no. 9 (Sept., 1958): 52.

37. Braybrook, "The Development of Synthetic Detergents," p. 406.

38. Morgan and Wizemann, "Growth of the Anionics," p. 51; John W. McCutcheon, "Synthetic Detergents: Main Types, Uses, Properties and Prospects," *Chemical Industries* 61, no. 5 (Nov., 1947): 811–24; John W. McCutcheon, "The

Retail Market for Synthetic Detergents," *Soap and Sanitary Chemicals* 24, no. 12 (Dec., 1948): 38.

39. Ross E. McKinney, "Syndets and Waste Disposal," *Sewage and Industrial Wastes* 29, no. 6 (June, 1957): 656.

Chapter II. The Foaming Problem: Eruption and Analysis

1. R. E. McKinney, "Syndets and Waste Disposal," *Sewage and Industrial Wastes* 29, no. 6 (June, 1957): 654.

2. Though soap's disposal had caused no problems, its manufacture had. "A characteristic of hard soap was that it was difficult to make unobtrusively. Clouds of steam and a distinctive smell were produced when it was boiled. . . ."—L. Gittins, "Soapmaking in Britain, 1824–1851: A Study in Industrial Location," *Journal of Historical Geography* 8, no. 1 (Jan., 1982): 30. Much more serious, the production of alkali (sodium carbonate) by the Leblanc process for use in soap, textile, and glass manufacture yielded hydrochloric acid gas as a byproduct. The deleterious effects of this byproduct on the local environments of James Muspratt's alkali plants in and near Liverpool, England, led to successful court actions against Muspratt. See Gordon W. Roderick and Michael D. Stephens, "Profits and Pollution: Some Problems Facing the Chemical Industry in the Nineteenth Century. The Corporation of Liverpool versus James Muspratt, Alkali Manufacturer, 1838," *Industrial Archaeology* 11, no. 2 (Spring, 1974): 35–45. In describing a second pollution problem caused by the manufacture of alkali, Roderick and Stephens quote J. M. Cohen, *Life of Ludwig Mond* (1956), pp. 74–75: "The alkali waste rich with extracted sulphur, choked the little streams that drained the marshland and polluted the Mersey itself. For every ton of soda made, approximately double its weight of Galligu—as it was called locally—a thick and evil-smelling mud, had to be dumped on the marsh and poured out on a waste land, whose purchase was always a problem to the alkali maker—but even when laid out on a waste land, from this nauseating sludge seeped the continual odor of rotten eggs. Finally, however, the stuff dried; and even then it remained a potent menace. For it was liable to heat in the sun, catch fire and give off the instant and corrosive gas, sulphur dioxide."

3. Joel A. Tarr, with James McCurley III, Francis C. McMichael, and Terry Yosie, "Water and Wastes: A Retrospective Assessment of Wastewater Technology in the United States, 1800–1932," *Technology and Culture* 25, no. 2 (Apr., 1984): 236.

4. Richard H. Bogan and Clair N. Sawyer, "Biochemical Degradation of Synthetic Detergents. I. Preliminary Studies," *Sewage and Industrial Wastes* 26, no. 9 (Sept., 1954): 1078.

5. "What Caused Suds in the Sewage Treatment Plant?" *American City* 62, no. 12 (Dec., 1947), p. 99.

6. There are two main methods or stages in sewage treatment. Primary treatment involves removing the grosser solids in sewage. Screens are used to remove such materials as sizable pieces of wood and plastic. The sewage is next allowed to flow through channels in which fast-settling grit is deposited while lighter solids are carried on. Considerable amounts of the latter are then removed by means of sedimentation in holding tanks. The effluent from primary treatment contains some suspended and much dissolved and colloidal matter. To remove this matter various methods of secondary treatment are used, among which trickling filters and the activated sludge pro-

cess are most common. A trickling filter has a bed, six to eight feet deep, consisting of stones two to four inches in diameter. Purification is carried out by bacteria living on the surfaces of the stones. The primary effluent is applied to the stones in a thin sheet or spray, usually from rotating arms onto a circular bed, with short intervals between applications, and allowed to trickle down through the bed. The activated-sludge method utilizes biologically active sludge mixed with the primary effluent and agitated in the presence of an ample supply of air in an aeration tank from four to ten hours. Suspended solids and many organic solids are quickly absorbed or adsorbed by the activated sludge, while organic matter is oxidized by the microorganisms in the sludge.

7. "More about Those Mt. Penn Suds," *American City* 63, no. 3, Mar., 1948, p. 111.

8. For details, see Thomas Whiteside, "Annals of Business: The Suds Conflict," *New Yorker* 40, Dec. 19, 1964, pp. 42ff. Whiteside argues that the promotion of the word *suds* into a synonym for cleanliness through three decades (1920s–40s) of advertising "represents an impressive achievement on the part of the soap industry" (p. 46).

9. "From Activated Sludge to Activated Suds at Batavia, Illinois," *Sewage and Industrial Wastes* 22, no. 3 (Mar., 1950): 362.

10. "Detergent Trouble," *American City* 65, no. 3, Mar., 1950, p. 13.

11. "The Problems of Detergents in Sanitary Engineering," *American City* 66, no. 9, Sept., 1951, p. 115; *Chemical and Engineering News* 29, no. 17 (Apr. 23, 1951): 1635–36.

12. Walter A. Sperry, "Detergents and Their Influence on Sewage Treatment," *Sewage and Industrial Wastes* 23, no. 12 (Dec., 1951): 1470.

13. W. N. Wells and C. H. Scherer, "Froth Formation and Synthetic Detergents," *Sewage and Industrial Wastes* 24, no. 5 (May, 1952): 672, 679.

14. Surfactants are classified according to whether or not they ionize in solution and by the nature of their ionic or electrical charges. Thus we have anionic, non-ionic, cationic, and amphoteric surfactants. An anionic surfactant is derived from an aliphatic hydrocarbon and usually a sodium salt in which the detergent and other properties depend in part on the negatively charged anion of the molecule. In the mid-nineteen-fifties the following chemical classifications of anionics existed: alkyl benzene sulfonates; normal fatty alcohol sulfates; secondary fatty alcohol sulfates; esters of sulfosuccinic acid; sulfated ethanol amides; sulfated monoglycerides; and miscellaneous petroleum sulfonates. Accounting for eighty per cent of total surfactant production, anionics were the most popular surfactants. The alkyl benzene sulfonates constituted sixty per cent, the fatty alcohol sulfates thirty per cent, and the remaining types ten per cent of total anionic production. See Ross E. McKinney, "Syndets and Waste Disposal," *Sewage and Industrial Wastes* 29, no. 6 (June, 1957): 655.

15. "Suds and Syndets," *Sewage and Industrial Wastes* 24, no. 5 (May, 1952): 682–83.

16. W. R. Gowdy, "Chemical Structure and Action of Synthetic Detergents," *Sewage and Industrial Wastes* 25, no. 1 (Jan., 1953): 19.

17. W. R. Gowdy, "Action of Detergents in Sewage Treatment—A Study by Industry," *Sewage and Industrial Wastes* 25, no. 3 (Mar., 1953): 255, 260.

18. Lawrence Flett and Lester F. Hoyt, "Detergent Compounds—Their Composition and Behavior," *Sewage and Industrial Wastes* 25, no. 3 (Mar., 1953): 251.

19. *Sewage and Industrial Wastes* 25, no. 3 (Mar., 1953): 254, 280.

20. "Effects of Synthetic Detergent Pollution," *Journal/American Water Works Association* 42, no. 1 (Jan., 1950): 17–25.

21. ORSANCO Detergent Subcommittee, "Components of Household Synthetic Detergents in Water and Sewage," *Journal/American Water Works Association* 55, no. 3 (Mar., 1963): 369.

22. A. R. Todd, "Water Purification Upset Seriously by Detergents," *Water and Sewage Works* 101, no. 2 (Feb., 1954): p. 80.

23. Eruptions of foam would continue to occur. For example, in Wisconsin alone the State Board of Health noted eleven instances on rivers and lakes and in one water filtration plant between 1950 and 1962. For details, see *Congressional Record*, 88th Cong., 1st sess., vol. 109, pt. 4, Mar. 25, 1963, pp. 4826–27.

24. William O. Lynch and Clair N. Sawyer, "Physical Behavior of Synthetic Detergents. I. Preliminary Studies on Frothing and Oxygen Transfer," *Sewage and Industrial Wastes* 26, no. 10 (Oct., 1954): 1193.

25. Ibid., p. 1199.

26. Ibid., p. 1200.

27. The biochemical oxygen demand (BOD) of domestic and industrial wastewaters is the amount of molecular oxygen required to stabilize the decomposable matter present in a water by aerobic biochemical action. The standard laboratory BOD test involves incubation for a period of five days at 20°C. The BOD test is among the most important made in sanitary analysis to determine the strength of wastewater. John W. Clark, Warren Viessman, Jr., and Mark J. Hammer, *Water Supply and Pollution Control*, 3d ed., p. 287. The Warburg respirometer is an apparatus of general utility in evaluating metabolic rates of microorganisms under a range of feed and environmental conditions. For further details and a sketch of the apparatus see: Richard A. Conway and Richard D. Ross, *Handbook of Industrial Waste Disposal*, pp. 141–42.

28. Richard H. Bogan and Clair N. Sawyer, "Biochemical Degradation of Synthetic Detergents. I. Preliminary Studies," *Sewage and Industrial Wastes* 26, no. 9 (Sept., 1954): 1070.

29. Included in this group were the alkyl sulfates, sulfonated fatty acid amides, sulfonated fatty acid esters, and certain fatty acid amides and esters of low molecular weight polyethylene glycols. Ibid., p. 1072.

30. This category included the alkyl benzene sulfonates, alkylnaphthalene sulfonate, the alkylphenoxy polyethylene oxide type, and derivatives of high molecular weight polyethylene glycols such as the amides, the esters, and the ethers. Ibid.

31. Ibid., p. 1076, 1080.

32. Richard H. Bogan and Clair N. Sawyer, "Biochemical Degradation of Synthetic Detergents. II. Studies on the Relation between Chemical Structure and Biochemical Oxidation," *Sewage and Industrial Wastes* 27, no. 8 (Aug., 1955): 917.

33. Ibid., p. 918.

34. C. Hammerton, "Observations on the Decay of Synthetic Anionic Detergents in Natural Waters," *Journal of Applied Chemistry* 5, no. 9 (Sept., 1955): 524.

35. Bogan and Sawyer, "Biochemical Degradation of Synthetic Detergents. II.," p. 924.

36. Ibid., p. 926.

37. Clair N. Sawyer, Richard H. Bogan, and James R. Simpson, "Biochemical Behavior of Synthetic Detergents," *Industrial and Engineering Chemistry* 48, no. 2 (Feb., 1956): 238.

38. Ibid., pp. 239, 240.

39. Richard H. Bogan and Clair N. Sawyer, "Biochemical Degradation of Synthetic Detergents. III. Relationships between Biological Degradation and Froth Persistence," *Sewage and Industrial Wastes* 28, no. 5 (May, 1956): 637–43.

40. Clair N. Sawyer and Devere W. Ryckman, "Anionic Synthetic Detergents and Water Supply Problems," *Journal/American Water Works Association* 49, no. 4 (Apr., 1957): 487; C. Hammerton, "Observations on the Decay of Synthetic Anionic Detergents in Natural Waters," *Journal of Applied Chemistry* 5, no. 9 (Sept., 1955): 517–24.

41. Sawyer and Ryckman, "Anionic Synthetic Detergents and Water Supply Problems," p. 487.

42. Clair N. Sawyer, "Effects of Synthetic Detergents on Sewage Treatment Processes," *Sewage and Industrial Wastes* 30, no. 6 (June, 1958): 771.

43. Ibid., pp. 772–73.

44. Sawyer's research assistants were R. H. Bogan, D. W. Ryckman, W. O. Lynch, P. L. McCarty, M. W. Pescod, P. C. Reist, and J. R. Simpson. Ibid., p. 774.

Chapter III. The Industry's Response to the Detergent Pollution Problem

1. ORSANCO Detergent Subcommittee, "Components of Household Synthetic Detergents in Water and Sewage," *Journal/American Water Works Association* 55, no. 3 (Mar., 1963): 369. This was the subcommittee's second report; its first was the source in note 3, below.

2. U.S. Department of Health, Education, and Welfare, *Proceedings: The National Conference on Water Pollution, December 12–14, 1960*, p. 271. For an account of the origins and activities of ORSANCO, see Edward J. Cleary, *The ORSANCO Story: Water Quality Management in the Ohio Valley Under an Interstate Compact.*

3. ORSANCO Chemical Industry Committee, "Detergents in Sewage and Surface Water," *Industrial Wastes* 1, no. 4 (July–Aug., 1956): 212–13.

4. Ibid., p. 212; F. J. Coughlin, "Detergents in Sewage," *Soap and Chemical Specialities* 32, no. 2 (Feb., 1956): 53. The U.S. Public Health Service, through the Taft Engineering Center in Cincinnati, Ohio, had informal ties with the analytic subcommittee.

5. American Water Works Association, Task Group, "Characteristics and Effects of Synthetic Detergents," *Journal/American Water Works Association* 46, no. 8 (Aug., 1954): 761. A widely used methylene blue extraction process was that described in P. N. Degens, Jr., H. Van Der Zee, and J. D. Kommer, "Anionic Syndets in Amsterdam Sewage," *Sewage and Industrial Wastes* 25, no. 1 (Jan., 1953): 20–25.

6. The Soap and Detergent Association, Technical Advisory Council, *Synthetic Detergents in Perspective: Their Relationship to Sewage Disposal and Safe Water Supplies,* p. 11. The AWWA task group's first report was "Characteristics and Effects of Synthetic Detergents," *Journal/American Water Works Association* 46, no. 8 (Aug., 1954): 751–74. It subsequently published "Effects of Synthetic Detergents on Water Supplies," Ibid. 49, no. 10 (Oct., 1957): 1355–58; and "Effects of Synthetic Detergents on Water Supplies," Ibid. 51, no. 10 (Oct., 1959): 1251–54.

7. Coughlin, "Detergents in Sewage," p. 53.

8. ORSANCO Detergent Subcommittee, "Components of Household Synthetic Detergents in Water and Sewage," p. 377.

9. Subcommittee on Analytical Methods, Technical Advisory Committee, Association of American Soap and Glycerine Producers, Inc., "Determination of Trace Amounts of Alkyl Benzenesulfonates in Water," *Analytical Chemistry* 28, no. 12 (Dec., 1956): 1822–26.

10. ORSANCO Detergent Subcommittee, "Components of Household Synthetic Detergents in Water and Sewage," p. 377.

11. Ibid.

12. ORSANCO Chemical Industry Committee, "Detergents in Sewage and Surface Water," p. 212.

13. P. J. Weaver, "Review of Detergent Research Program," *Journal of the Water Pollution Control Federation* 32, no. 3 (Mar., 1960): p. 289.

14. Coughlin, "Detergents in Sewage," p. 69. The AASGP was formed in 1926. By 1963, soon after it had changed its name to the Soap and Detergent Association, it had as members almost 120 manufacturers, including producers of household detergents, producers of cleaning products for industry and institutions, makers of glycerine and fatty acids, and suppliers of basic chemicals to detergent producers. The firms ranged in size from very large corporate complexes to small specialty producers.

15. The ABS used in the studies was a composite ABS made from the products of the four ABS suppliers represented on the research steering committee.

16. W. K. Griesinger, "Detergents in Sewage and Water Treatment Plants," *Soap and Chemical Specialties* 37, no. 3 (Mar., 1961): p. 50.

17. Coughlin, "Detergents in Sewage," p. 69.

18. Ross E. McKinney and James M. Symons, "Bacterial Degradation of ABS. I. Fundamental Biochemistry," *Sewage and Industrial Wastes* 31, no. 5 (May, 1959): 549, 553, 554, 555.

19. C. N. Sawyer and D. W. Ryckman, "Anionic Synthetic Detergents and Water Supply Problems," *Journal/American Water Works Association* 49, no. 4 (Apr., 1957): 480. See discussion of Sawyer and Ryckman in previous chapter.

20. McKinney and Symons, "Bacterial Degradation of ABS. I. Fundamental Biochemistry," p. 551.

21. Weaver, "Review of Detergent Research Program," p. 289.

22. W. K. Griesinger, "Detergents in Sewage and Water Treatment Plants," *Soap and Chemical Specialties* 37, no. 3 (Mar., 1961): 48.

23. J. David Justice, "Detergents in Water Pollution," *Soap and Chemical Specialities* 38, no. 3 (Mar., 1962): 51.

24. Ross E. McKinney and Eugene J. Donovan, "Bacterial Degradation of ABS. II. Complete Mixing Activated Sludge," *Sewage and Industrial Wastes* 31, no. 6 (June, 1959): 690.

25. Ibid., p. 695.

26. Weaver, "Review of Detergent Research Program," p. 293.

27. Coughlin, "Detergents in Sewage," p. 53; Ralph House and B. A. Fries, "Radioactive ABS in Activated Sludge Sewage Treatment," *Sewage and Industrial Wastes* 28, no. 4 (Apr., 1956): 492–506.

28. Coughlin, "Detergents in Sewage," p. 69.

29. P. H. McGauhey and Stephen A. Klein, "Removal of ABS by Sewage Treatment," *Sewage and Industrial Wastes* 31, no. 7 (Aug., 1959): 882.

30. Ibid., p. 885.

31. P. H. McGauhey and Stephen A. Klein, "The Removal of ABS from Sewage," *Public Works Magazine* 92, no. 5 (May, 1961): 102.

32. Ibid., p. 103.

33. Ibid., p. 104.

34. F. J. Coughlin, "Soap Manufacturers' Report of Research on Synthetic Detergents," *Journal/American Water Works Association* 48, no. 1 (Jan., 1956): 74; W. R. Gowdy, "Chemical Structure and Action of Synthetic Detergents," *Sewage and Industrial Wastes* 25, no. 1 (Jan., 1953): 15–19.

35. L. B. Polkowski, G. A. Rohlich, and J. R. Simpson, "Evaluation of Frothing in Sewage Treatment Plants," *Sewage and Industrial Wastes* 31, no. 9 (Sept., 1959): 1013; Coughlin, "Soap Manufacturers' Report of Research on Synthetic Detergents," p. 74.

36. James J. Morgan and Richard S. Engelbrecht, "Survey of Phosphate and ABS Concentrations in Illinois Streams," *Journal/American Water Works Association* 52, no. 4 (Apr., 1960): 471.

37. Ibid., p. 482.

38. Weaver, "Review of Detergent Research Program," p. 295. The average concentration of surface-active agents in the Ohio River at Cincinnati, based on weekly analyses with the methylene blue procedure from 1955 through 1959, was found to be 0.16 ppm, measured as "apparent ABS." During this period there was no increase or buildup of the apparent ABS content. See Paul J. Weaver and Francis J. Coughlin, "Monitoring the Ohio River for Synthetic-Detergent Content," *Journal/American Water Works Association* 52, no. 5 (May, 1960): 607–12.

39. Charles E. Renn and Mary F. Barada, "Adsorption of ABS on Particulate Materials in Water," *Sewage and Industrial Wastes* 31, no. 7 (July, 1959): 850–54.

40. W. J. Payne, "Synthetic Detergents in Water and Sewage Systems," *Science* 139, no. 3551 (Jan. 18, 1963): 198; Weaver, "Review of detergent research program," p. 295.

41. Charles E. Renn and Mary F. Barada, "Removal of ABS from Heavily Polluted Waters," *Journal/American Water Works Association* 53, no. 12 (Feb., 1961): 129.

42. Jesse M. Cohen, "Syndets in Water Supplies," *Soap and Chemical Specialities* 35, no. 9 (Sept., 1959): 56.

43. John M. Flynn, Aldo Andreoli, and August A. Guerrera, "Study of Synthetic Detergents in Ground Water," *Journal/American Water Works Association* 50, no. 2 (Dec., 1958): 1553–54.

44. *New York Times,* Aug. 17, 1958, p. 62.

45. Flynn, Andreoli, and Guerrera, "Study of Synthetic Detergents in Ground Water," p. 1557.

46. Ibid., p. 1559.

47. *New York Times,* Jan. 6, 1960, p. 43.

48. *New York Times,* Dec. 12, 1961, p. 45.

49. *New York Times,* Apr. 20, 1962, p. 29.

50. *Time* 79, no. 18 (May 4, 1962), p. 68.

51. Graham Walton, "ABS Contamination," *Journal/American Water Works Association* 52, no. 11 (Nov., 1960): 1357.

52. Jerome Deluty, "Synthetic Detergents in Well Water," *Public Health Reports* 75, no. 1 (Jan., 1960): 75.

53. M. Starr Nichols and Elaine Koepp, "Synthetic Detergents as a Criterion of Wisconsin Ground Water Pollution," *Journal/American Water Works Association* 53, no. 3 (Mar., 1961): 306.

54. Frank L. Woodward, Franklin J. Kilpatrick, and Paul B. Johnson, "Experi-

ences with Ground Water Contamination in Unsewered Areas in Minnesota," *American Journal of Public Health* 51, no. 8 (Aug., 1961): 1132–33.

55. *New York Times,* Nov. 15, 1963, p. 21.

56. Another, though much less serious, problem reported in 1959 was the backing up of suds in the drains of apartment houses. The AASGP's research steering committee created a plumbing subcommittee to study the problem. J. David Justice, "Detergents in Water and Sewage," *Soap and Chemical Specialties,* 36, no. 7 (July, 1960): 57.

57. S. Freeman et al., "The Enzyme-inhibiting Action of an Alkyl Aryl Sulfonate and Studies on its Toxicity when Ingested by Rats, Dogs and Humans," *Gastroenterology* 4,(1945): 332.

58. Research Steering Committee of the Technical Advisory Council of the Association of American Soap and Glycerine Producers, Inc., "ABS and the Safety of Water Supplies," *Journal/American Water Works Association* 52, no. 6 (June, 1960): 789.

59. T. W. Tusing, O. E. Paynter, and D. L. Opdyke, "The Chronic Toxicity of Sodium Alkylbenzenesulfonate by Food and Water Administration to Rats," *Toxicology and Applied Pharmacology* 2, (1960): 464–73.

60. Ibid., p. 473. A related study was also carried out at Hazleton Laboratories by O. E. Paynter and Robert J. Weir, Jr., "Chronic Toxicity of Santomerse No. 3 from Olefin (Dodecyl Benzene Sodium Sulfonate)," *Toxicology and Applied Pharmacology* 2, (1960): 641–48. Dodecyl benzene sodium sulfonate was widely used as an emulsifying, wetting, and spreading agent for fungicidal and insecticidal sprays and dustsprays; it was used also in washing spray residues from fruit. The objective of the investigation was to appraise the hazard involved in the ingestion of small residues of dodecyl benzene sodium sulfonate that might remain on unrinsed fruits, vegetables, and other edible products. The surfactant was fed to rats over a two-year period at levels up to two thousand ppm. Again, no adverse effects were observed.

61. W. K. Griesinger, "Detergents in Sewage and Water Treatment Plants," *Soap and Chemical Specialities* 37, no. 3 (Mar., 1961): 50.

62. W. K. Griesinger, "Role of ABS in Water Pollution," *Soap and Chemical Specialities* 39, no. 4 (Apr., 1963): 44.

63. Association of American Soap and Glycerine Producers, "Occurrence of ABS in Water Supplies," *Journal/American Water Works Association* 53, no. 3 (Mar., 1961): 297–300.

64. Omar C. Hopkins and Oscar Gullans, "New USPHS Standards," *Journal/American Water Works Association* 52, no. 9 (Sept., 1960): 1166–67; ORSANCO Detergent Subcommittee, "Components of Household Synthetic Detergents in Water and Sewage," *Journal/American Water Works Association* 55, no. 3 (Mar., 1963): 383. It may be of interest to note that at dishwashing or laundering concentrations, ABS was present at 400 to 600 ppm.

65. U.S. Department of Health, Education, and Welfare, *Public Health Service Drinking Water Standards,* rev. ed., p. 24. Although the report stated the levels of pollution were "questionable," there was in fact no scientific reason to label them as such.

66. Floyd B. Taylor,"Effectiveness of Water Utility Quality Control Practices," *Journal/American Water Works Association* 54, no. 10 (Oct., 1962): 1260.

67. U.S. Department of Health, Education, and Welfare, *Clean Water: A Challenge to the Nation. Highlights and Recommendations of the National Conference on*

Water Pollution p. 7; Graham Walton, "ABS Contamination," *Journal/American Water Works Association* 52, no. 11 (Nov., 1960): 1354.

68. ORSANCO Detergent Subcommittee, "Components of Household Synthetic Detergents in Water and Sewage," pp. 380–81; W. K. Griesinger, "Detergents in Sewage and Water Treatment Plants," *Soap and Chemical Specialities* 37, no. 3 (Mar., 1961): 50.

69. W. K. Griesinger, "Role of ABS in Water Pollution," *Soap and Chemical Specialties* 39, no. 4 (Apr., 1963): 43–44.

70. Jesse M. Cohen, "Taste and Odor of ABS in Water," *Journal/American Water Works Association* 55, no. 5 (May, 1963): 590.

71. W. K. Griesinger, "Detergents in Sewage and Water Treatment Plants," *Soap and Chemical Specialities* 37, no. 3 (Mar., 1961): 51.

72. G. G. Robeck, A. R. Bryant, and R. L. Woodward, "Influence of ABS on Coliform Movement through Water-saturated Sandy Soils," *Journal/American Water Works Association* 54, no. 1 (Jan., 1962): 81.

73. W. J. Payne, "Synthetic Detergents in Water and Sewage Systems," p. 197.

74. P. J. Weaver, "Review of Detergent Research Program," *Journal of the Water Pollution Control Federation* 32, no. 3 (Mar., 1960): 295.

75. ORSANCO Detergent Subcommittee, "Components of Household Synthetic Detergents in Water and Sewage," *Journal/American Water Works Association* 55, no. 3 (Mar., 1963): 395.

76. U.S. Department of Health, Education, and Welfare, *Clean Water: A Challenge to the Nation*, p. 39.

77. J. David Justice, "Detergents in Water Pollution," *Soap and Chemical Specialties* 38, no. 3 (Mar., 1962): 51.

78. Ibid., p. 52; Technical Advisory Council, Soap and Detergent Association, *Synthetic Detergents in Perspective: Their Relationship to Sewage Disposal and Safe Water Supplies*, p. 11; F. J. Coughlin, "Detergents and Water Pollution Abatement," *American Journal of Public Health* 55, no. 5 (May 1965): 765.

79. U.S. Department of Health, Education, and Welfare, *Proceedings: The National Conference on Water Pollution, December 12–14, 1960*, p. 457.

80. Ibid., p. 459.

81. Technical Advisory Council, Soap and Detergent Association, *Synthetic Detergents in Perspective*, p. 30.

82. W. J. Payne, "Synthetic Detergents in Water and Sewage Systems," p. 197.

83. *New York Times*, May 19, 1963, p. 86.

Chapter IV. The British Experience with Synthetic Detergents

1. *Times*, Jan. 12, 1953, p. 7.

2. *Times*, Jan. 23, 1953, p. 3.

3. *Times*, Jan. 24, 1953, pp. 3, 7.

4. U.K., Ministry of Housing and Local Government, *Interim Report of the Committee on Synthetic Detergents*, p. 2. The committee was chaired by Sir Harry Jephcott, Chairman and Managing Director, Glaxo Laboratories Ltd. Its governmental members were: N. R. Beattie, Principal Medical Officer, Ministry of Health; C. E. Boast, formerly Borough Engineer and Surveyor, Croydon Borough Council; G.

MacRobbie, Assistant Secretary, Department of Health for Scotland; J. R. Nicholls, formerly Deputy Government Chemist; F. T. K. Pentelow, Chief Inspector of Salmon and Freshwater Fisheries, Ministry of Agriculture, Fisheries and Food; B. A. Southgate, Director of Water Pollution Research, Department of Scientific and Industrial Research; J. H. Street, Under Secretary, Ministry of Housing and Local Government; C. B. Townend, Chief Engineer, Middlesex County Council Main Drainage Department; and E. Windle Taylor, Director of Water Examination, Metropolitan Water Board. Representing industry were: G. H. W. Cullinan, Commercial Director, Shell Chemical Company Ltd.; R. H. Greenly, Director, Thomas Hedley and Company Ltd.; F. D. Morrell, Director, Unilever Ltd.; and W. L. Thomas, Chief Chemist and Technical Director, Woolcombers Ltd. The sole academic representative was J. C. Cruickshank, Professor of Bacteriology as Applied to Hygiene, London School of Hygiene and Tropical Medicine.

5. U.K., Ministry of Housing and Local Government, *Report of the Committee on Synthetic Detergents*, p. 1.

6. Ibid., pp. 9, 10.

7. Ibid., p. 11.

8. Ibid., pp. 15, 17–18.

9. Ibid., pp. 17, 22.

10. Ibid., pp. 24, 25.

11. Ibid., p. 28.

12. Ibid., pp. 31, 32.

13. Ibid., pp. 34, 35.

14. Ibid., pp. 39–40, 43.

15. Ibid., p. 48.

16. Ibid.

17. Ibid., p. 51.

18. U.K., Ministry of Housing and Local Government, *Progress Report of the Standing Technical Committee on Synthetic Detergents*, p. 2. The committee's chair was H. W. Cremer, Senior Partner, Cremer and Brearley, Consulting Engineers. Members included: N. R. Beattie, Principal Medical Officer, Ministry of Health; E. A. B. Birse, Chief Chemical Inspector, Department of Health for Scotland; A. H. Cook, Assistant Director, Brewing Industry Research Foundation; A. Key, Senior Chemical Inspector, Ministry of Housing and Local Government; J. Longwell, Deputy Government Chemist, Department of Scientific and Industrial Research; F. T. K. Pentelow, Chief Inspector of Salmon and Freshwater Fisheries, Ministry of Agriculture, Fisheries and Food; B. A. Southgate, Director of Water Pollution Research, Department of Scientific and Industrial Research; R. C. Tarring, a Shell Chemical Company scientist; and E. Windle Taylor, Director of Water Examination, Metropolitan Water Board. Of the remaining six members of the committee—R. C. Dickie, H. R. Galleymore, W. E. Hamer, G. C. Hampson, S. H. Jenkins, and D. H. A. Price—all but the first were scientists, four of them being fellows of the Royal Institute of Chemistry.

19. R. C. Tarring, "The Development of a Biologically Degradable Alkyl Benzene Sulphonate," *International Journal of Air and Water Pollution* 9 (1965): 546, 548.

20. Surfactants with the trade name "Dobane" possessed a near C_{12} alkyl group.

21. U.K., Ministry of Housing and Local Government, *Second Progress Report of the Standing Technical Committee on Synthetic Detergents*, pp. 7–8.

22. C. A. Houston, "Foreign Requirements and Developments in Biodegradability," *Journal of the American Oil Chemists' Society* 40, no. 11 (Nov., 1963): 660.

23. U.K., Ministry of Housing and Local Government, *Second Progress Report of the Standing Technical Committee on Synthetic Detergents*, pp. 8, 9.

24. U.K., Ministry of Housing and Local Government, *Third Progress Report of the Standing Technical Committee on Synthetic Detergents*, p. 7.

25. Ibid., p. 9.

26. U.K., Ministry of Housing and Local Government, *Fourth Progress Report of the Standing Technical Committee on Synthetic Detergents*, p. 5.

27. Ibid., pp. 8, 17.

28. U.K., Ministry of Housing and Local Government, *Fifth Progress Report of the Standing Technical Committee on Synthetic Detergents*, p. 6.

29. Ibid.; U.K., Ministry of Housing and Local Government, *Sixth Progress Report of the Standing Technical Committee on Synthetic Detergents*, p. 6.

30. U.K., Ministry of Housing and Local Government, *Sixth Progress Report of the Standing Technical Committee on Synthetic Detergents*, p. 7; Tarring, "The Development of a Biologically Degradable Alkyl Benzene Sulphonate," p. 551.

31. U.K., Ministry of Housing and Local Government, *Sixth Progress Report of the Standing Technical Committee on Synthetic Detergents*, p. 6.

32. Ibid., p. 8.

33. Ibid., p. 9.

34. These figures differ somewhat from those (from 3 to about 1.3 ppm) given in the committee's 1961 report.

35. U.K. Ministry of Housing and Local Government, *Sixth Progress Report of the Standing Technical Committee on Synthetic Detergents*, p. 10.

Chapter V. U.S. Government Response to the Detergent Pollution Problem

1. Federal Republic of Germany, Ministry of Health, "Development of the Detergent Problem in the Federal Republic of Germany," in U.S. Congress, Senate, *Water Pollution Control*, Hearings before a Special Subcommittee on Air and Water Pollution of the Committee on Public Works, 88th Cong., 1st sess. (June 17, 18, 19, 20, 25, and 26, 1963), p. 350.

2. John Moser, vice president and director of Lever Brothers, ibid., p. 686.

3. "German Firm Develops New Syndets," *Chemical and Engineering News* 41, no. 8 (Feb. 25, 1963): 55.

4. Federal Republic of Germany, Ministry of Health, "Development of the Detergent Problem in the Federal Republic of Germany," in U.S. Congress, House, *Water Pollution Control*, Hearings before a Special Subcommittee on Air and Water Pollution of the Committee on Public Works, 88th Cong., 1st sess. (June 17, 18, 19, 20, 25, and 26, 1963), p. 351.

5. Edward Wise, "Detergents—A Source of Pollution and What Is Being Done," ibid., p. 671. For the text of the law see Appendix I, esp. article 1.1.

6. Appendix I, article 2.1.

7. For details, see "Syndet Testing Could Follow German Lead," *Chemical and Engineering News* 41, no. 7 (Feb. 18, 1963): 65–66.

8. Federal Republic of Germany, Ministry of Health, "Development of the Detergent Problem in the Federal Republic of Germany," in U.S. Congress, Senate, *Water Pollution Control*, Hearings before a Special Subcommittee on Air and Water Pollu-

tion of the Committee on Public Works, 88th Cong., 1st sess. (June 17, 18, 19, 20, 25, and 26, 1963), p. 351; "German Firm Develops New Syndets," *Chemical and Engineering News* 41, no. 8 (Feb. 25, 1963): 55.

9. U.S. Congress, House, *Water Pollution Control Act Amendments,* Hearings before the Committee on Public Works, 88th Cong., 1st sess. (Dec. 4, 5, 6, 9, and 10, 1963), 2d sess. (Feb. 4, 5, 6, 7, 18, and 19, 1964), p. 171; U.S. Congress, Senate, *Water Pollution Control,* Hearings before a Special Subcommittee on Air and Water Pollution of the Committee on Public Works, 88th Cong., 1st sess. (June 17, 18, 19, 20, 25, and 26, 1963), p. 343.

10. *Congressional Record,* 88th Cong., 1st sess., Jan. 17, 1963, vol. 109, pt. 1, p. 560.

11. Edward Wise, "Detergents—A Source of Pollution and What Is Being Done," in U.S. Congress, House, *Water Pollution Control and Abatement (Part 1B—National Survey),* Hearings before the Natural Resources and Power Subcommittee of the Committee on Government Operations, 88th Cong., 1st sess. (June 6, 10, 11, 12, 13, 14, 18, 20, and 25, 1963), p. 1003.

12. U.S. Congress, House, *Water Pollution Control Act Amendments,* Hearings before the Committee on Public Works, 88th Cong., 1st sess. (Dec. 4, 5, 6, 9, and 10, 1963), 2d sess. (Feb. 4, 5, 6, 7, 18, and 19, 1964), p. 171.

13. Wise, "Detergents—A Source of Pollution and What Is Being Done," pp. 1011, 1013.

14. *Congressional Record,* 88th Cong., 1st sess., Jan. 17, 1963, vol. 109, pt. 1, p. 558 (for the full text of H.R. 2105 see Appendix II); ibid., Feb. 11, 1963, pt. 2, p. 2216. Reuss should have said "surface-active agents" rather than "surface-active detergents."

15. Ibid., Jan. 17, 1963, pt. 1, p. 558.

16. Ibid., pp. 559, 560. Syndets do dissolve in water; Reuss meant "degrade."

17. During the 1970s, several years after the surfactant problem had been solved, U.S. public health officials became concerned that the sodium salt of nitrilotriacetic acid, used as a builder in detergents, might be carcinogenic, and discouraged its use.

18. Ibid., p. 560; ibid., June 10, 1963, pt. 8, p. 10527.

19. Ibid., Jan. 17, 1963, pt. 1, p. 560.

20. Ibid., Feb. 11, 1963, pt. 2, p. 2216.

21. Ibid., p. 2215.

22. *Chemical and Engineering News* 41, no. 11 (Mar. 18, 1963): 111.

23. For the full text of H.R. 4571 see Appendix II.

24. *Congressional Record,* 88th Cong., 1st sess., Mar. 19, 1963, vol. 109, pt. 4, p. 4473.

25. Ibid., Mar. 25, 1963, p. 4826.

26. Ibid., p. 4834.

27. Ibid., pp. 4826, 4827.

28. Before the end of the 1960s a strong environmental movement had formed in Wisconsin in connection with a much more harmful pollutant, DDT. Thomas R. Dunlap, *DDT: Scientists, Citizens, and Public Policy,* p. 161.

29. John H. Fenton, *Midwest Politics,* pp. 57, 74.

30. Robert C. Nesbit, *Wisconsin: A History,* p. 507.

31. American Water Works Association, Task Group 2661 P, "Evaluation of Legislation to Control Detergents," *Journal/American Water Works Association* 55, no. 10 (Oct., 1963): 1232; *Journal, Water Pollution Control Federation* 35, no. 7 (July, 1963): 949.

32. *Chemical and Engineering News* 41, no. 11 (Mar. 18, 1963): 111.

33. Ibid., p. 112.

34. *Water Pollution Control and Abatement (Part 1B—National Survey)* Hearings before the Natural Resources and Power Subcommittee of the Committee on Government Operations, U.S. House of Representatives, 88th Cong., 1st sess. (June 6, 10, 11, 12, 13, 14, 18, 20, and 25, 1963), p. 1102.

35. As quoted by Reuss, *Congressional Record,* 88th Cong., 1st sess., June 10, 1963, vol. 108, pt. 8, p. 10528.

36. Ibid.

37. U.S. Congress, House, *Water Pollution Control and Abatement (Part 1B— National Survey),* Hearings before the Natural Resources and Power Subcommittee of the Committee on Government Operations, 88th Cong., 1st sess. (June 6, 10, 11, 12, 13, 14, 18, 20, and 25, 1963), pp. 982, 984.

38. *Congressional Record,* 88th Cong., 1st sess., May 13, 1963, vol. 109, pt. 6, p. 8369.

39. U.S. Congress, House, *Water Pollution Control and Abatement (Part 1B— National Survey),* Hearings before the Natural Resources and Power Subcommittee of the Committee on Government Operations, 88th Cong., 1st sess. (June 6, 10, 11, 12, 13, 14, 18, 20, and 25, 1963), p. 1045.

40. Ibid., p. 1046.

41. Ibid., pp. 1048, 1051.

42. Ibid., pp. 1055, 1056.

43. Ibid., pp. 1060, 1100.

44. Ibid., p. 1102.

45. Ibid., p. 1118.

46. *Congressional Record,* 88th Cong., 1st sess., Oct. 16, 1963, vol. 109, pt. 15, p. 19661; for the full text of the bill see: U.S. Congress, Senate, *Water Pollution Control,* Hearings before a Special Subcommittee on Air and Water Pollution of the Committee on Public Works, 88th Cong., 1st sess. (June 17, 18, 19, 20, 25, and 26, 1963), pp. 3–5; J. Clarence Davies III and Barbara S. Davies, *The Politics of Pollution,* 2d ed., pp. 32–33.

47. U.S. Congress, Senate, *Water Pollution Control,* Hearings before a Special Subcommittee on Air and Water Pollution of the Committee on Public Works, 88th Cong., 1st sess. (June 17, 18, 19, 20, 25, and 26, 1963), p. 651.

48. Ibid., pp. 652, 654.

49. Ibid., p. 658.

50. Samuel P. Hays, *Beauty, Health, and Permanence: Environmental Politics in the United States, 1955–1985,* p. 53.

51. U.S. Congress, Senate, *Water Pollution Control,* Hearings before a Special Subcommittee on Air and Water Pollution of the Committee on Public Works, 88th Cong., 1st sess. (June 17, 18, 19, 20, 25, and 26, 1963), p. 658.

52. Ibid., p. 659.

53. Ibid.

54. Ibid., pp. 682–83.

55. Ibid., p. 692.

56. Ibid., p. 693.

57. American Water Works Association, Task Group, "Evaluation of Legislation to Control Synthetic Detergents," *Journal/American Water Works Association* 55, no. 10 (Oct., 1963): 1233.

58. Ibid., pp. 1234, 1235.

59. "AWWA Rejects Ban on Hard Detergents," *American City* 78, no. 7 (July, 1963): 123.

60. U.S. Congress, Senate, Committee on Public Works, *Federal Water Pollution Control Act Amendments of 1963,* Report no. 556 to Accompany S.649, 88th Cong., 1st sess., 1963, p. 10.

61. *Congressional Record,* 88th Cong., 1st sess., Oct. 16, 1963, vol. 109, pt. 15, p. 19675.

62. Ibid., Oct. 17, 1963, p. 19820.

63. *New York Times,* Dec. 19, 1963, p. 34.

64. U.S. Congress, House, *Water Pollution Control Act Amendments,* Hearings before the Committee on Public Works, 88th Cong., 1st sess. (Dec. 4, 5, 6, 9, 10, 1963), 2d sess. (Feb. 4, 5, 6, 7, 18, 19, 1964), pp. 88–89.

65. Ibid., pp. 94–95, 137–39, 151–54.

66. Ibid., p. 150.

67. Ibid., p. 146.

68. Ibid., p. 155.

69. Ibid., p. 174.

70. Ibid., pp. 445–50.

71. Ibid., p. 448.

72. Ibid., p. 450.

73. U.S. Congress, House, Committee on Public Works, *Federal Water Pollution Control Act Amendments,* Report no. 1885 to Accompany S.649, 88th Cong., 2d sess., 1964, p. 7.

74. Ibid., p. 6.

75. The House failed to take final action before the 88th Congress adjourned. At the beginning of the next Congress, in January 1965, Muskie introduced a new bill containing the same provisions and again the Senate passed it. This time the House acted, passing an amended version of the bill. On October 2, 1965, President Johnson signed into law the Water Quality Act of 1965. See Davies and Davies, *The Politics of Pollution,* pp. 33–34.

76. Arnold J. Heidenheimer, Hugh Heclo, and Carolyn Teich Adams, *Comparative Public Policy: The Politics of Social Choice in Europe and America,* 2d ed., p. 17.

Chapter VI. Fashioning an Acceptable Surfactant

1. U.S. Congress, Senate, *Water Pollution,* Hearings before a Special Subcommittee on Air and Water Pollution of the Committee on Public Works, 89th Cong., 1st sess., Part I, General hearings held on progress and programs relating to the abatement of water pollution (May 19, 20, and 21, 1965), p. 175. The Monsanto Company, a supplier of primary materials, itself had tested some 450 products: U.S. Congress, Senate, *Water Pollution Control,* Hearings before a Special Subcommittee on Air and Water Pollution of the Committee on Public Works, 88th Cong., 1st sess. (June 17, 18, 19, 20, 25, and 26, 1963), p. 647.

2. A. Davidsohn and B. M. Milwidsky, *Synthetic Detergents,* 5th ed., p. 6.

3. U.S. Congress, Senate, *Water Pollution,* Hearings before a Special Subcommittee on Air and Water Pollution of the Committee on Public Works, 89th Cong.,

1st sess., Part I, General hearings held on progress and programs relating to the abatement of water pollution (May 19, 20, and 21, 1965), p. 175.

4. *Chemical and Engineering News* 41, no. 11 (Mar. 18, 1963): 106–107.

5. D. Justice and V. Lamberti, "Revolution in Detergents," *Chemical Engineering Progress* 60, no. 12 (Dec., 1964): 39. Another source—*Chemical and Engineering News* 41, no. 44 (Nov. 4, 1963): 139—stated: "In a typical cracking, 100 lb. of paraffin yield about 35 lb. of gas, 5 lb. of aromatics, 5 lb. of paraffins, and 55 lb. of olefins. Of the olefins, about 18 lb. are C_4 to C_7, 18 lb. are C_8 to C_{13}, and 19 lb. are C_{14} to C_{22}. Of the olefins, about 85% are alpha olefins." The olefins form a family of unsaturated, chemically active hydrocarbons (C_nH_{2n}) with one carbon-carbon double bond. In an alpha-olefin the double bond is at the alpha position, that is, between an end carbon and its neighbor carbon.

6. The alkylation of benzene by a linear olefin, alpha-dodecene, for example, gave rise to the following components for the production of linear alkyl sulfonate:

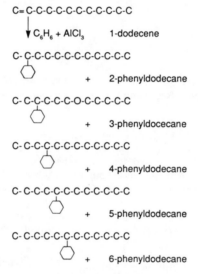

Alternatively, producing normal alcohols from the olefins could lead to alcohol sulfates, alcohol ethoxylates, or alcohol ethoxylate sulfate; while producing linear alkyl phenols could lead to normal alkyl phenol ethoxylate or normal alkyl phenol ethoxylate sulfate. R. D. Swisher, "LAS: Major Development in Detergents," *Chemical Engineering Progress* 60, no. 12 (Dec., 1964): 41; "Impact of Technology on Surface Active Agents Market," *Soap and Chemical Specialities* 40, no. 9 (Sept., 1964): 68.

7. U.S. Congress, Senate, *Water Pollution Control,* Hearings before a Special Subcommittee on Air and Water Pollution of the Committee on Public Works, 88th Cong., 1st sess. (June 17, 18, 19, 20, 25, and 26, 1963), p. 648.

8. *Chemical and Engineering News* 41, no. 11 (Mar. 18, 1963): 102.

9. "ABS Study Reveals Effect of Syndet Structure," *Chemical and Engineering News* 41, no. 22 (June 3, 1963): 70–71.

10. The first step in this process was a growth step in which ethylene was built up in a random manner on aluminum-triethyl to give a higher aluminum-trialkyl:

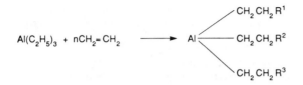

The higher aluminum-trialkyl was then subjected to a displacement reaction involving additional ethylene in the presence of cobalt, nickel, or platinum as catalyst. This yielded higher alpha-olefins, and regenerated the aluminum-triethyl:

$$Al \begin{cases} CH_2CH_2R^1 \\ CH_2CH_2R^2 + 3CH_2=CH_2 \\ CH_2CH_2R^3 \end{cases} \longrightarrow R^1CH=CH_2 + R^2CH=CH_2 + R^3CH=CH_2 + Al(C_2H_5)_3$$

One of these alpha-olefins could, for example, have been alpha-dodecene, which reacts with benzene as indicated earlier. Justice and Lamberti, "Revolution in Detergents," p. 38; *Chemical and Engineering News* 41, no. 44 (Nov. 4, 1963): 139.

11. Ibid. no. 11 (Mar. 18, 1963): 102.

12. Ibid. p. 106. A normal-paraffin is a member of the methane series of hydrocarbons (C_nH_{2n+2}) having all its carbon atoms arranged in a single straight chain.

13. Ibid. no. 24 (June 17, 1963): 25.

14. *Water Pollution Control*, Hearings before a Special Subcommittee on Air and Water Pollution of the Committee on Public Works, U.S. Senate, 88th Cong., 1st sess., (June 17, 18, 19, 20, 25, and 26, 1963), p. 644; *Chemical and Engineering News* 41, no. 24 (June 17, 1963): 25.

15. *Chemical and Engineering News* 41, no. 44 (Nov. 4, 1963): 138.

16. *Chemical Week* 94, no. 22 (May 30, 1964): 115; *Chemical and Engineering News* 41, no. 44 (Nov. 4, 1963): 139; Justice and Lamberti, "Revolution in Detergents," p. 39.

17. Justice and Lamberti, "Revolution in Detergents," p. 36.

18. Charles K. Hersh, *Molecular Sieves*, p. 4.

19. "Impact of Technology on Surface Active Agents Market," *Soap and Chemical Specialties* 40, no. 9 (Sept., 1964): 69.

20. *Chemical and Engineering News* 40, no. 40 (Oct. 29, 1962): 17; ibid. no. 11 (Mar. 18, 1963): 106.

21. U.S. Congress, Senate, *Water Pollution Control,* Hearings before a Special Subcommittee on Air and Water Pollution of the Committee on Public Works, 88th Cong., 1st sess. (June 17, 18, 19, 20, 25, and 26, 1963), p. 354.

22. Justice and Lamberti, "Revolution in Detergents," p. 36.

23. Ibid., p. 37.

24. Ibid.; Hersh, *Molecular Sieves,* pp. 107–108.

25. John Winton, "The Detergent Revolution," *Chemical Week* 94, no. 22 (May 30, 1964): 121, 122.

26. Normal-paraffins could be converted into several useful biodegradable surfactants. But most importantly they could be monochlorinated ($C_{12}H_{26} + Cl_2 \rightarrow C_{12}H_{25}Cl + HCl$), and then either reacted directly with benzene using aluminum trich-

loride as a catalyst or first dehydrochlorinated to give random olefins ($C_{12}H_{25}Cl \rightarrow C_{12}H_{24} + HCl$), which could then be used to alkylate benzene. Sulfonation of the resulting linear alkylbenzene with either sulfur trioxide or oleum gave rise to LAS. Justice and Lamberti, "Revolution in Detergents," p. 38.

27. Henry V. Moss, Monsanto Chemical Company, in U.S. Congress, Senate, *Water Pollution Control,* Hearings before a Special Subcommittee on Air and Water Pollution of the Committee on Public Works, 88th Cong., 1st sess. (June 17, 18, 19, 20, 25, and 26, 1963), pp. 646–48.

28. Soon after work began on the development of more highly biodegradable surfactants, it became apparent that standardization of methodology would be necessary to assure a uniform evaluation of the many materials under test in the various companies. In 1961 the Technical Advisory Committee of the Soap and Detergent Association established the Subcommittee on Biodegradation Test Methods. The committee charged the subcommittee with reviewing and evaluating existing procedures, and with developing, if necessary, new methods and standards to meet the industry's needs. The subcommittee subsequently published "A Procedure and Standards for the Determination of the Biodegradability of Alkyl Benzene Sulfonate and Linear Alkylate Sulfonate," *Journal of the American Oil Chemists' Society* 42, no. 11 (Nov., 1965): 986–93.

29. U.S. Congress, Senate, *Water Pollution Control,* Hearings before a Special Subcommittee on Air and Water Pollution of the Committee on Public Works, 88th Cong., 1st sess. (June 17, 18, 19, 20, 25, and 26, 1963), pp. 650, 679.

30. U.S. Congress, House, *Water Pollution Control Act Amendments,* Hearings before the Committee on Public Works, 88th Cong., 1st sess. (Dec. 4, 5, 6, 9, and 10, 1963), 2d sess. (Feb. 4, 5, 6, 7, 18, and 19, 1964), pp. 445–50.

31. U.S. Congress, Senate, *Water Pollution,* Hearings before a Special Subcommittee on Air and Water Pollution of the Committee on Public Works, 89th Cong., 1st sess., Part I, General hearings held on progress and programs relating to the abatement of water pollution (May 19, 20, and 21, 1965), p. 159.

32. *Chemical and Engineering News* 45, no. 9 (Feb. 27, 1967): 21.

33. Ibid., p. 20.

Epilogue. The Problem Solved: Biodegradable LAS

1. *Congressional Record,* 89th Cong., Mar. 10, 1965, vol. 111, pt. 4, p. 4589.

2. Ibid.

3. U.S. Congress, Senate, *Water Pollution,* Hearings before a Special Committee on Air and Water Pollution of the Committee on Public Works, 89th Cong., 1st sess., Part I, General hearings held on progress and programs relating to the abatement of water pollution (May 19, 20, and 21, 1965), p. 159.

4. Ibid., p. 161.

5. Ibid., p. 179.

6. Ibid., pp. 180, 182.

7. Ibid., p. 182.

8. Ibid., pp. 185–6, 189.

9. U.S. Congress, Senate, *Water Pollution Control—1966,* Hearings before the Subcommittee on Air and Water Pollution of the Committee on Public Works, 89th Cong., 2d sess. (Apr. 19, 20, 26, 27, 28; May 5, 10, 11, and 12, 1966), p. 567.

10. Ibid., p. 369.

11. Ibid., pp. 595, 606.

12. Ibid., p. 594.

13. Bernard L. Oser and Kenneth Morgareidge, "Toxicologic Studies with Branched and Linear Alkyl Benzene Sulfonates in Rats," *Toxicology and Applied Pharmacology* 7 (1965): 819–25.

14. U.S. Congress, Senate, *Water Pollution Control—1966*, Hearings before the Subcommittee on Air and Water Pollution of the Committee on Public Works, 89th Cong., 2d sess., (Apr. 19, 20, 27, 28; May 5, 10, 11, and 12, 1966), pp. 571, 595, 596, 605.

15. Ibid., pp. 595, 567.

16. *Chemical and Engineering News* 45, no. 9 (Feb. 27, 1967): 20.

17. W. Husmann, "Solving the Detergent Problem in Germany," *Water Pollution Control* 67, (1968): 81–83.

18. D. H. A. Price, "Pollution by Synthetic Detergents: Towards a Solution," *Water Pollution Control* 67 (1968): 56, 57.

19. T. Waldmeyer, "Analytical Records of Synthetic Detergent Concentrations, 1956–1966: A Ten-year Success Story," *Water Pollution Control* 67 (1968): 66.

Bibliography

"ABS Study Reveals Effect of Syndet Structure." *Chemical and Engineering News* 41, no. 22 (June 3, 1963): 70–71.

"AWWA Rejects Ban on Hard Detergents." *American City* 78, no. 7 (July, 1963): pp. 123–28.

American Water Works Association, Task Group. "Characteristics and Effects of Synthetic Detergents." *Journal/American Water Works Association* 46, no. 8 (August, 1954): 751–74.

———. "Effects of Synthetic Detergents on Water Supplies." *Journal/American Water Works Association* 49, no. 10 (October, 1957): 1355–58.

———. "Effects of Synthetic Detergents on Water Supplies." *Journal/American Water Works Association* 51, no. 10 (October, 1959): 1251–54.

American Water Works Association, Task Group 2661 P. "Evaluation of Legislation to Control Detergents." *Journal/American Water Works Association* 55, no 10 (October, 1963): 1229–34.

Association of American Soap and Glycerine Producers. "Occurrence of ABS in Water Supplies." *Journal/American Water Works Association* 53, no. 3 (March, 1961): 297–300.

Bogan, Richard H., and Clair N. Sawyer. "Biochemical Degradation of Synthetic Detergents. I. Preliminary Studies." *Sewage and Industrial Wastes* 26, no. 9 (September, 1954): 1069–80.

———. "Biochemical Degradation of Synthetic Detergents. III. Relationships between Biological Degradation and Froth Persistence." *Sewage and Industrial Wastes* 28, no. 5 (May, 1956): 637–43.

———. "Biochemical Degradation of Synthetic Detergents. II. Studies on the Relation between Chemical Structure and Biochemical Oxidation." *Sewage and Industrial Wastes* 27, no. 8 (August, 1955): 917–28.

Braybrook, F. H. "The Development of Synthetic Detergents and Future Trends." *Chemistry and Industry* (June 26, 1948): 404–407, 409.

Chemical and Engineering News. April 23, 1951, pp. 1635–36. October 29, 1962, p. 17. March 18, 1963, pp. 102–108, 110–12, 114, 126. June 17, 1963, pp. 25–26. November 4, 1963, pp. 138–41. February 27, 1967, pp. 20–21.

Chemical Week, May 30, 1964, pp. 111–26.

Clark, John W., Warren Viessman, Jr., and Mark H. Hammer. *Water Supply and Pollution Control,* 3d ed. New York: Harper and Row, 1977.

Cleary, Edward J. *The ORSANCO Story: Water Quality Management in the Ohio Valley Under an Interstate Compact.* Baltimore, Md: The Johns Hopkins Press, 1967.

Cohen, Jesse M. "Syndets in Water Supplies." *Soap and Chemical Specialities* 35, no. 9 (September, 1959): 53–56, 119, 121.

———. "Taste and Odor of ABS in Water." *Journal/American Water Works Association* 55, no. 5 (May, 1963): 587–91.

Commoner, Barry. *The Closing Circle: Nature, Man and Technology.* New York: Alfred A. Knopf, 1971.

———. "A Reporter at Large: The Environment." *New Yorker,* June 15, 1987, pp. 46–47, 50–54, 56–71.

Congressional Record. 88th Cong., 1st sess., January 17, 1963. Vol. 109, pt. 1, pp. 558–62.

Congressional Record. 88th Cong., 1st sess., March 19, 1963. Vol. 109, pt. 4, pp. 4473.

Congressional Record. 88th Cong., 1st sess., March 25, 1963. Vol. 109, pt. 4, pp. 4826–38.

Congressional Record. 88th Cong., 1st sess., May 13, 1963. Vol. 109, pt. 6, pp. 8368–69.

Congressional Record. 88th Cong., 1st sess., June 10, 1963. Vol. 109, pt. 8, pp. 10527–28.

Congressional Record. 88th Cong., 1st sess., October 16, 1963. Vol. 109, pt. 15, pp. 19661–82.

Congressional Record. 89th Cong., 1st sess., March 10, 1965. Vol. 111, pt. 4, pp. 4587–90.

Conway, Richard A., and Richard D. Ross. *Handbook of Industrial Waste Disposal.* New York: Van Nostrand Reinhold Company, 1980.

Coughlin, F. J. "Detergents and Water Pollution Abatement." *American Journal of Public Health* 55, no. 5 (May, 1965): 760–71.

———. "Detergents in Sewage." *Soap and Chemical Specialities* 32, no. 2 (February, 1956): 51–53, 67, 69, 71.

———. "Soap Manufacturers' Report of Research on Synthetic Detergents." *Journal/ American Water Works Association,* 48, no. 1 (January, 1956): 70–74.

Davidsohn, A., and B. M. Milwidsky. *Synthetic Detergents,* 5th ed. London: Leonard Hill, 1972.

Davies, J. Clarence III, and Barbara S. Davies. *The Politics of Pollution,* 2d ed. Indianapolis: Pegasus. The Bobbs-Merrill Company, 1975.

Degens, P. N., Jr., H. Van Der Zee, and J. D. Kommer. "Anionic Syndets in Amsterdam Sewage." *Sewage and Industrial Wastes* 25, no. 1 (January, 1953): 20–25.

Deluty, Jerome. "Synthetic Detergents in Well Water." *Public Health Reports* 75, no. 1 (January, 1960): 75–77.

"Detergent Trouble." *American City* 65, no. 3 (March, 1950): 13.

"'Dreft' Led the Way." *Soap and Chemical Specialities* 34, no. 9 (September, 1958): 47–50, 121.

Dunlap, Thomas R. *DDT: Scientists, Citizens, and Public Policy.* Princeton, New Jersey: Princeton University Press, 1981.

Dworsky, Leonard B. *Pollution.* Vol. 1 of *Conservation in the United States: A Documentary History.* Edited by Frank E. Smith. New York: Chelsea House Publishers, 1971.

"Effects of Synthetic Detergent Pollution." *Journal/American Water Works Association* 42, no. 1 (January, 1950): 17–25.

Fenton, John H. *Midwest Politics.* New York: Holt, Rinehart and Winston, 1966.

Flett, Lawrence, and Lester F. Hoyt. "Detergent Compounds—Their Composition and Behavior," *Sewage and Industrial Wastes* 25, no. 3 (March, 1953): 245–51.

Flynn, John M., Aldo Andreoli, and August A. Guerrera. "Study of Synthetic Detergents in Ground Water." *Journal/American Water Works Association* 50, no. 12 (December, 1958): 1551–62.

Freeman, S., et al. "The Enzyme-inhibiting Action of an Alkyl Aryl Sulfonate and Studies on Its Toxicity When Ingested by Rats, Dogs and Humans." *Gastroenterology* 4 (1945): 332–43.

"From Activated Sludge to Activated Suds at Batavia, Illinois." *Sewage and Industrial Wastes* 22, no. 3 (March, 1950): 362–65.

"German Firm Develops New Syndets." *Chemical and Engineering News* 41, no. 8 (February 25, 1963): 55–56.

Gibbs, F. W. "The History of the Manufacture of Soap." *Annals of Science* 4 (1939): 169–90.

Gittins, L. "Soapmaking in Britain, 1824–1851: A Study in Industrial Location." *Journal of Historical Geography* 8, no. 1 (January, 1982): 29–40.

Gowdy, W. R. "Action of Detergents in Sewage Treatment—A Study by Industry." *Sewage and Industrial Wastes* 25, no. 3 (March, 1953): 255–60.

———. "Chemical Structure and Action of Synthetic Detergents." *Sewage and Industrial Wastes* 25, no. 1 (January, 1953): 15–19.

Griesinger, W. K. "Detergents in Sewage and Water Treatment Plants." *Soap and Chemical Specialities* 37, no. 3 (March, 1961): 48–51, 103.

———. "Role of ABS in Water Pollution." *Soap and Chemical Specialities* 39, no. 4 (April, 1963): 43–45.

Hammerton, C. "Observations on the Decay of Synthetic Anionic Detergents in Natural Waters." *Journal of Applied Chemistry* 5, no. 9 (September, 1955): 517–24.

Hays, Samuel P. *Beauty, Health, and Permanence: Environmental Politics in the United States, 1955–1985.* Cambridge: Cambridge University Press, 1987.

———. "From Conservation to Environment: Environmental Politics in the United States Since World War Two." *Environmental Review* 6, no. 2 (Fall, 1982): 14–41.

Heidenheimer, Arnold J., Hugh Heclo, and Carolyn Teich Adams. *Comparative Public Policy: The Politics of Social Choice in Europe and America,* 2d ed. New York: St. Martin's Press, 1983.

Hersberger, A. B., and C. P. Neidig. "Present Status of Organic Synthetic Detergents." *Chemical and Engineering News* 27, no. 23 (June 6, 1949): 1646–50.

Hersh, Charles K. *Molecular Sieves.* New York: Reinhold Publishing Corporation, 1961.

Hopkins, Omar C., and Oscar Gullans. "New USPHS Standards." *Journal/American Water Works Association* 52, no. 9 (September, 1960): 1161–68.

House, Ralph, and B. A. Fries. "Radioactive ABS in Activated Sludge Sewage Treatment." *Sewage and Industrial Wastes* 28, no. 4 (April, 1956): 492–506.

Houston, C. A. "Foreign Requirements and Developments in Biodegradability." *Journal of the American Oil Chemists' Society* 40, no. 11 (November, 1963): 659–60.

Husmann, W. "Solving the Detergent Problem in Germany." *Water Pollution Control* 67 (1968): 80–83.

"Impact of Technology on Surface Active Agents Market." *Soap and Chemical Specialities* 40, no. 9 (September, 1964): 67–70, 128–29.

Johnson, H. C. E. "Is Soap Slipping?" *Scientific American,* August, 1946, pp. 57–59.

Journal, Water Pollution Control Federation 35, no. 7 (July, 1963): 949.

Justice, J. David. "Detergents in Water and Sewage." *Soap and Chemical Specialities* 36, no. 7 (July, 1960): 55–57, 174–75.

———. "Detergents in Water Pollution." *Soap and Chemical Specialities* 38, no. 3 (March, 1962): 51–53, 95.

Justice, D., and V. Lamberti. "Revolution in Detergents." *Chemical Engineering Progress* 60, no. 12 (December, 1964): 35–40.

Kastens, Merritt L., and Jackson J. Ayo, Jr. "Pioneer Surfactant." *Industrial and Engineering Chemistry* 42, no. 9 (September, 1950): 1626–38.

Kushner, Laurence M., and James I. Hoffman. "Synthetic Detergents." *Scientific American,* October, 1951, pp. 26–30.

Larson, T. E. "Synthetic Detergents." *Journal/American Water Works Association* 41, no. 4 (April, 1949): 315–21.

Lawless, Edward W. *Technology and Social Shock.* New Brunswick, New Jersey: Rutgers University Press, 1977.

Levitt, Benjamin. *Oils, Detergents and Maintenance Specialities.* New York: Chemical Publishing Co., 1967.

Longman, G. F. *The Analysis of Detergents and Detergent Products.* London: John Wiley and Son, 1975.

Lynch, William O., and Clair N. Sawyer. "Physical Behavior of Synthetic Detergents. I. Preliminary Studies on Frothing and Oxygen Transfer." *Sewage and Industrial Wastes* 26, no. 10 (October, 1954): 1193–1201.

Mazur, Allan. *The Dynamics of Technical Controversy.* Washington, D.C.: Communications Press, 1981.

McCutcheon, John W. "The Retail Market for Synthetic Detergents." *Soap and Sanitary Chemicals* 24, no. 12 (December, 1948): 37–39, 155.

———. *Synthetic Detergents.* New York: MacNair-Dorland Company, 1950.

———. "Synthetic Detergents: Main Types, Uses, Properties and Prospects." *Chemical Industries* 61, no. 5 (November, 1947): 811–24.

McGauhey, P. H., and Stephen A. Klein. "Removal of ABS by Sewage Treatment." *Sewage and Industrial Wastes* 31, no. 7 (August, 1959): 877–99.

———. "The Removal of ABS from Sewage." *Public Works Magazine* 92, no. 5 (May, 1961): 101–104.

McGucken, William. *Scientists, Society, and State: The Social Relations of Science Movement in Great Britain, 1931–1947.* Columbus: Ohio State University Press, 1984.

McKinney, Ross E. "Syndets and Waste Disposal." *Sewage and Industrial Wastes* 29, no. 6 (June, 1957): 654–66.

McKinney, Ross E., and Eugene J. Donovan. "Bacterial Degradation of ABS. II. Complete Mixing Activated Sludge." *Sewage and Industrial Wastes,* 31, no. 6 (June, 1959): 690–96.

McKinney, Ross E., and James M. Symons. "Bacterial Degradation of ABS. I. Fundamental Biochemistry." *Sewage and Industrial Wastes* 31, no. 5 (May, 1959): 549–56.

Molliet, J. L., B. Collie, and W. Black. *Surface Activity: The Physical Chemistry, Technical Applications, and Chemical Constitution of Synthetic Surface-active Agents,* 2d ed. Princeton, New Jersey: Van Nostrand, 1961.

"More about those Mt. Penn Suds." *American City* 63, no. 3 (March, 1948): 111.

Morgan, O. M., and Leslie C. Wizemann. "Growth of the Anionics." *Soap and Chemical Specialities* 34, no. 9 (September, 1958): 51–53.

Morgan, James J., and Richard S. Engelbrecht. "Survey of Phosphate and ABS Concentrations in Illinois Streams." *Journal/American Water Works Association* 52, no. 4 (April, 1960): 471–82.

Nelkin, Dorothy, and Michael Pollack. *The Atom Besieged: Extraparliamentary Dissent in France and Germany.* Cambridge, Massachusetts: The MIT Press, 1981.

Nesbit, Robert C. *Wisconsin: A History.* Madison: University of Wisconsin Press, 1973.

New York Times, October 15, 1948. August 17, 1958. January 6, 1960. December 12, 1961. April 20, 1962. May 19, 1963. November 15, 1963. December 19, 1963.

Nichols, M. Starr, and Elaine Koepp. "Synthetic Detergents as a Criterion of Wisconsin Ground Water Pollution." *Journal/American Water Works Association* 53, no. 3 (March, 1961): 303–306.

ORSANCO Chemical Industry Committee. "Detergents in Sewage and Surface Water." *Industrial Wastes* 1, no. 4 (July–August, 1956): 212–13.

———. "Components of Household Synthetic Detergents in Water and Sewage." *Journal/American Water Works Association* 55, no. 3 (March, 1963): 369–402.

Oser, Bernard L., and Kenneth Morgareidge. "Toxicologic Studies with Branched and Linear Alkyl Benzene Sulfonates in Rats." *Toxicology and Applied Pharmacology* 7 (1965): 819–25.

Payne, W. J. "Synthetic Detergents in Water and Sewage Systems." *Science,* January 18, 1963, pp. 197–98.

Paynter, O. E., and Robert J. Weir, Jr. "Chronic Toxicity of Santomerse No. 3. from Olefin (Dodecyl Benzene Sodium Sulfonate)." *Toxicology and Applied Pharmacology* 2 (1960): 641–48.

Polkowski, L. B., G. A. Rohlich, and J. R. Simpson. "Evaluation of Frothing in Sewage Treatment Plants." *Sewage and Industrial Wastes* 31, no. 9 (September, 1959): 1004–15.

Price, D. H. A. "Pollution by Synthetic Detergents: Towards a Solution," *Water Pollution Control* 67 (1968): 56–58.

Price, Donald. *Detergents: What They Are and What They Do.* New York: Chemical Publishing Co., 1952.

"The Problems of Detergents in Sanitary Engineering." *American City* 66, no. 9 (September, 1951): 115.

"A Procedure and Standards for the Determination of the Biodegradability of Alkyl Benzene Sulfonate and Linear Alkylate Sulfonate." *Journal of the American Oil Chemists' Society* 42, no. 11 (November, 1965): 986–93.

Renn, Charles E., and Mary F. Barada. "Absorption of ABS on Particulate Materials in Water." *Sewage and Industrial Wastes* 31, no. 7 (July, 1959): 850–54.

————. "Removal of ABS from Heavily Polluted Waters." *Journal/American Water Works Association* 53, no. 2 (February, 1961): 129–34.

Research Steering Committee of the Technical Advisory Council of the Association of American Soap and Glycerine Producers, Inc. "ABS and the Safety of Water Supplies." *Journal/American Water Works Association* 52, no. 6 (June, 1960): 786–90.

Robeck, G. G., A. R. Bryant, and R. L. Woodward. "Influence of ABS on Coliform Movement through Water-saturated Sandy Soils." *Journal/American Water Works Association* 54, no. 1 (January, 1962): 75–82.

Roderick, Gordon W., and Michael D. Stephens. "Profits and Pollution: Some Problems Facing the Chemical Industry in the Nineteenth Century. The Corporation of Liverpool versus James Muspratt, Alkali Manufacturer, 1838." *Industrial Archaeology* 11, no. 2 (Spring, 1974): 35–45.

Sawyer, Clair N. "Effects of Synthetic Detergents on Sewage Treatment Processes." *Sewage and Industrial Wastes* 30, no. 6 (June, 1958): 757–75.

Sawyer, Clair N., and Devere W. Ryckman. "Anionic Synthetic Detergents and Water Supply Problems." *Journal/American Water Works Association* 49, no. 4 (April, 1957): 480–90.

Sawyer, Clair N., Richard H. Bogan, and James R. Simpson. "Biochemical Behavior of Synthetic Detergents." *Industrial and Engineering Chemistry* 48, no. 2 (February, 1956): 236–40.

Schisgall, Oscar. *Eyes on Tomorrow: The Evolution of Procter and Gamble.* Chicago: J. G. Ferguson Publishing Company, 1981.

Sewage and Industrial Wastes 25, no. 3 (March, 1953): 252–54.

Shreve, R. Norris. *Chemical Process Industries,* 3d ed. New York: McGraw Hill Book Co., 1967.

Simcox, A. K. "The Future of Synthetic Detergents in Relation to the Petroleum-Chemical Industry." *Chemistry and Industry* (March 11, 1950): 178–82.

Singer, Charles, et al., eds. *A History of Technology.* 8 vols. Oxford: Clarendon Press, 1954–1978.

The Soap and Detergent Association, Technical Advisory Council. *Synthetic Deter-*

gents in Perspective: Their Relationship to Sewage Disposal and Safe Water Supplies. New York: Soap and Detergent Association, 1962.

Sperry, Walter A. "Detergents and Their Influence on Sewage Treatment." *Sewage and Industrial Wastes* 23, no. 12 (December, 1951): 1469–76.

Subcommittee on Analytical Methods, Technical Advisory Committee, Association of American Soap and Glycerine Producers. "Determination of Trace Amounts of Alkyl Benzenesulfonates in Water." *Analytical Chemistry* 28, no. 12 (December, 1956): 1822–26.

"Suds and Syndets." *Sewage and Industrial Wastes* 24, no. 5 (May, 1952): 682–83.

Swisher, R. D. "LAS: Major Development in Detergents." *Chemical Engineering Progress* 60, no. 12 (December, 1964): 41–45.

"Syndet Testing Could Follow German Lead." *Chemical and Engineering News* 41, no. 7 (February 18, 1963): 65–66.

Tarr, Joel A. "Industrial Wastes and Public Health: Some Historical Notes, Part I, 1876–1932." *American Journal of Public Health* 75, no. 9 (September, 1985): 1059–67.

————. "The Search for the Ultimate Sink: Urban Air, Land, and Water Pollution in Historical Perspective." *Records of the Columbia Historical Society of Washington, D.C.* 51, (1984): 1–29.

————. "The Separate vs. Combined Sewer Problem: A Case Study in Urban Technology Design Choice." *Journal of Urban History* 5, no. 3 (May, 1979): 308–39.

Tarr, Joel A., James McCurley III, Francis C. McMichael, and Terry Yosie. "Water and Wastes: A Retrospective Assessment of Wastewater Technology in the United States, 1800–1932." *Technology and Culture* 25, no. 2 (April, 1984): 226–63.

Tarr, Joel A., and Francis Clay McMichael. "Decisions about Wastewater Technology: 1850–1932." *Journal of the Water Resources Planning and Management Division, Proceedings of the American Society of Civil Engineers* 103, no. WR1 (May, 1977): 47–61.

Tarr, Joel A., Francis C. McMichael, et al. "Retrospective Assessment of Waste Water Technology in the United States: 1800–1972." A Report to the National Science Foundation/RANN, Carnegie-Mellon University, October 1977.

Tarr, Joel A., Terry Yosie, and James McCurley III. "Disputes over Water Quality Policy: Professional Cultures in Conflict, 1900–1917." *American Journal of Public Health,* 70 no. 4 (April, 1980): 427–35.

Tarring, R. C. "The Development of a Biologically Degradable Alkyl Benzene Sulphonate," *International Journal of Air and Water Pollution* 9 (1965): 545–52.

Taylor, Floyd B. "Effectiveness of Water Utility Quality Control Practices." *Journal/ American Water Works Association,* 54 no. 10 (October, 1962): 1257–64.

Technical Advisory Council, Soap and Detergent Association. *Synthetic Detergents in Perspective.* New York: Soap and Detergent Association, 1962.

Technical Advisory Council, Soap and Detergent Association. *Synthetic Detergents in Perspective: Their Relationship to Sewage Disposal and Safe Water Supplies.* New York: Soap and Detergent Association, 1962.

Time, May 4, 1962, p. 68.

Times. January 12, 23, 24, 1953.

Todd, A. R. "Water Purification Upset Seriously by Detergents." *Water and Sewage Works* 101, no. 2 (February, 1954): 80.

Tusing, T. W., O. E. Paynter, and D. L. Opdyke. "The Chronic Toxicity of Sodim Alkylbenzenesulfonate by Food and Water Administration to Rates." *Toxicology and Applied Pharmacology* 2 (1960): 464–73.

U.K., Ministry of Housing and Local Government. *Fifth Progress Report of the Standing Technical Committee on Synthetic Detergents.* London: H.M.S.O., 1962.

———. *Fourth Progress Report of the Standing Technical Committee on Synthetic Detergents.* London: H.M.S.O., 1961.

———. *Interim Report of the Committee on Synthetic Detergents.* London: H.M.S.O., 1954.

———. *Progress Report of the Standing Technical Committee on Synthetic Detergents.* London: H.M.S.O., 1958.

———. *Report of the Committee on Synthetic Detergents.* London: H.M.S.O., 1956.

———. *Second Progress Report of the Standing Technical Committee on Synthetic Detergents.* London: H.M.S.O., 1959.

———. *Sixth Progress Report of the Standing Technical Committee on Synthetic Detergents.* London: H.M.S.O., 1963.

———. *Third Progress Report of the Standing Technical Committee on Synthetic Detergents.* London: H.M.S.O., 1960.

U.S. Congress, House. *Water Pollution Control Act Amendments,* Hearings before the Committee on Public Works. 88th Cong., 1st sess., December 4, 5, 6, 9, and 10, 1963; 2d. sess., February 4, 5, 6, 7, 18, and 19, 1964.

———. *Water Pollution Control and Abatement (Part 1B—National Survey),* Hearings before the Natural Resources and Power Subcommittee of the Committee on Government Operations. 88th Cong., 1st sess., June 6, 10, 11, 12, 13, 14, 18, 20, and 25, 1963.

———. Committee on Public Works. *Federal Water Pollution Control Act Amendments,* Report no. 1885 to Accompany S.649. 88th Cong., 2d sess., 1964.

U.S. Congress, Senate. *Water Pollution,* Hearings before a Special Subcommittee on Air and Water Pollution of the Committee on Public Works. 89th Cong., 1st sess., Part I, General hearings held on progress and programs relating to the abatement of water pollution, May 19, 20, and 21, 1965.

———. *Water Pollution Control,* Hearings before a Special Subcommittee on Air and Water Pollution of the Committee on Public Works. 88th Cong., 1st sess., June 17, 18, 19, 20, 25, and 26, 1963.

———. *Water Pollution Control—1966,* Hearings before the Subcommittee on Air and Water Pollution of the Committee on Public Works. 89th Cong., 2d sess., April 19, 20, 26, 27, 28; May 5, 10, 11, and 12, 1966.

———. Committee on Public Works. *Federal Water Pollution Control Act Amendments of 1963,* Report no. 556 to Accompany S.649. 88th Cong., 1st sess., 1963.

U.S. Department of Health, Education, and Welfare. *Clean Water: A Challenge to the Nation. Highlights and Recommendations of the National Conference on Water Pollution.* Washington, D.C.: Government Printing Office, 1961.

———. *Proceedings: The National Conference on Water Pollution,* December 12–14, 1960. Washington, D.C.: Government Printing Office, 1961.

———. *Public Health Service Drinking Water Standards. Revised 1962*. Washington, D.C.: U.S. Government Printing Office, 1962.

Waldmeyer, T. "Analytical Records of Synthetic Detergent Concentrations, 1956–1966. A Ten-Year Success Story." *Water Pollution Control* 67 (1968): 66–79.

Walton, Graham. "ABS Contamination." *Journal/American Water Works Association* 52, no. 11 (November, 1960): 1354–62.

Weaver, P. J. "Review of Detergent Research Program." *Journal of the Water Pollution Control Federation* 32, no. 3 (March, 1960): 288–96.

Weaver, Paul J., and Francis J. Coughlin. "Monitoring the Ohio River for Synthetic Detergent Content," *Journal/American Water Works Association* 52, no. 5 (May 1960): 607–12.

Wells, W. N., and C. H. Scherer. "Froth Formation and Synthetic Detergents." *Sewage and Industrial Wastes* 24, no. 5 (May, 1952): 670–79.

"What Caused Suds in the Sewage Treatment Plant?" *American City* 62, no. 12 (December, 1947): 99.

Whiteside, Thomas. "Annals of Business: The Suds Conflict." *New Yorker,* December 19, 1964, pp. 42–46, 48, 50, 53–55, 59–60, 62, 65.

Wilson, Charles. *The History of Unilever: A Study in Economic Growth and Social Change*. New York: Frederick A. Praeger, Publishers, 1968.

Winton, John. "The Detergent Revolution." *Chemical Week* 94, no. 22 (May 30, 1964): 111–26.

Woodward, Frank, Franklin J. Kilpatrick, and Paul B. Johnson. "Experiences with Ground Water Contamination in Unsewered Areas in Minnesota." *American Journal of Public Health* 51, no. 8 (August, 1961): 1130–36.

Index

Biodegradable was composed into type on a Linotron 202 phototypesetter in ten point Times Roman with two points of spacing between the lines. Times Roman was also selected for display. The book was designed by Susan Pearce, typeset by Graphic Composition, Inc., printed offset by Thomson-Shore, Inc., and bound by John H. Dekker & Sons, Inc. The paper on which this book is printed carries acid-free characteristics for an effective life of at least three hundred years.

TEXAS A & M UNIVERSITY PRESS : COLLEGE STATION